CHASING THE HORIZON

MARK CHENEY

Published 2016 by arima publishing

www.arimapublishing.com

ISBN 978 1 84549 690 6

© Mark Cheney 2016

All rights reserved

This book is copyright. Subject to statutory exception and to provisions of relevant collective licensing agreements, no part of this publication may be reproduced, stored in a retrieval system, or transmitted in any form or by any means, without the prior written permission of the author.

Printed and bound in the United Kingdom

Typeset in Garamond

This book is sold subject to the conditions that it shall not, by way of trade or otherwise, be lent, re-sold, hired out, or otherwise circulated without the publisher's prior consent in any form of binding or cover other than that which it is published and without a similar condition including this condition being imposed on the subsequent purchaser.

Swirl is an imprint of arima publishing.

arima publishing
ASK House, Northgate Avenue
Bury St Edmunds, Suffolk IP32 6BB
t: (+44) 01284 700321

www.arimapublishing.com

INTRODUCTION

A 1988 VW transporter played a great part in my recovery, about the same time I discovered my camper I started to ride my motorbike once again. Determination, change, you think how can I improve that? What can I do to make things work for me? To make life easier. Must I be at home by 2pm every day?

No an old VW Camper will help. Little did I know it would totally change my life. Improve my life with a great deal of trials, heart ache and pleasure. Taking me to so many places that I never dreamt I would ever visit again. My camper became a love affair, a friend and finally a rocket ship.

I found love, I am so sorry.

My thanks to Susan who without her assistance I could not have completed my book.

To my children who without their support I do not think I would have made it.

Thanks to my Mum and Dad, from whom determination and pioneering must have evolved.

To my uncle who recently passed away.

Thank you.

To Jenny who finally gave up saying sorry.

FINDING MY WAY

I cannot walk up hill, I cannot walk down hill, and I haven't the stamina. I am getting stronger but it is so slow.

What do they mean, you're doing well? You are taken to a swimming pool, yes you are swimming again, you go to the café after your swim, but have to look at the wall (why?). You cannot stand the speed of the people around you coming and going and their constant chatter. You get home and you sleep for four hours. You go to bed at night and sleep all night. Life seems to revolve around sleeping. What's happened to me, why can't I work this out?

You can make a cup of tea and boil an egg (so you are cooking again) you made a big meal last week (well I think it was last week) beans on toast. You did not wash the plate or cup, you smashed them against the wall. What did your Occupational Therapist say, how wonderful, what an achievement! What are they talking about?

You are unable to see the improvements you are making. I see now that there was great improvement but for quite a few years I had no idea. You cannot see that you are alive, you could have died, and that you never think about. You do not appreciate what gains you are making because you only think of what you could do before you had your head nearly hit off by 2 cwt. of steel. You know you are angered but why? I do not know I have forgotten. Why can't I have a complete day out? Why do I get so tired? Why do I always have to sleep in the afternoon?

Very slowly I became aware that I had sustained a very bad head injury but would forget everything ten minutes later. It was going to be a long time before I could stay out for a day.

There had been various suggestions as to how I could get around my afternoon sleeping. The less understanding few suggested well just do not go to bed, not very smart. Just have a cat nap in the chair, not very smart when I sleep I sleep for four hours. That is not a cat nap.

Well just work your way through it, no, no, no can't you see that will not work.

How can I get my head around this?

MY HOTEL ON WHEELS

Out of the blue it came to me, if I had a van, maybe I could sleep in the back. I could put a mattress down to sleep on, then drive home. That way I could have a day out and not have to be home by lunch time.

Well this seemed to be an idea worth thinking about. I made a note on my Filofax that I must try and get a van long enough for me to sleep in the back.

One morning some weeks later, I was driving through a local town and because of road works I had to take a detour around the houses. I saw to my delight this blue VW van which was parked on my right hand side. I parked behind it (it) fancy calling it, it. The tyres were flat, the paint work was very dull but to my delight there was a for sale sign in the window.

For sale, I searched for a pen, nothing, finally I found a stone and scratched the phone number onto it. Right, now have a look around it. Um it is quite old, it looks as if it has been partly converted to a camper (even better). With my stone carefully stored away I was on my way home. During my recovery I had also become very impulsive. I found later on if I could hang on for a couple of days then the impulsion would become less of a problem but for now I must get home to ring this number.

I did not realise what this little van had in store for me, or I for it. What IT again no, no it is going to be my camper. (Impulsive again). Now home I dialled the number scratched on my stone, Cotswold stone of course, (how posh am I?). It rang and rang Oooohhhh finally, "Hello, I saw your van and I wondered if it's still for sale?" "YES" was the reply. "Well good, can I come and have a look?" "Yes can you come on Saturday at 10.30am?" "Fine I will see you then."

Quite thrilled I rang a friend called Nick who I know has had VW's like this one for some years. "What year is it?" "1988." "Oh getting on a bit." "Well yes." "You do know they are gutless." "Really?" "Yes, afraid so." "Oh well I conveniently forgot about that, impulse had kicked in but they were quite well made and there are a lot about. "Is it a flat four?" "No idea?" "Well they are o.k., easy to repair when they blow up." "Blow up?" "Well you know they split between the valves." Pooh this sounds wonderful but they are a good van. "Just don't touch it if it's got rust in the chassis." "Well how am I going to know this, can you come with me to look at it?" "No sorry, I booked mine in to have some welding done." Why did I ring him?

Well I must face this alone. My Son did say he would come with me if he could get back in time.

On thinking about the transporter, my Dad at some time had a blue transporter and from what I remember it was a very nice one. What engine was fitted I have no idea, but they did get away in it quite often. I remember him saying it was a bit big for them. This I could not see, to me they seemed to be about the right size. I think they went to Ireland but my Mother had not been well for some years, after the marriage had become a little difficult. That seemed to have been rectified, but I believe my mother never fully recovered and they did return early.

CAN I OWN A T25

I rested most of the week to enable me to be as alert as one could be.

Saturday arrived and putting £500-00 in my pocket I took the same route as before. To my pleasant surprise there was this very shiny van with fully inflated tyres. The owner was still working away on the van. I parked and walked over to him "Hello." "Good morning" was the reply. "Well you have been busy." "Yes it just needed a good clean." "Well you have certainly done that."

"Do you know anything about these vans?" "No" I said. "Well it is a 1988 VW transporter, this one has a 1600cc turbo diesel engine" "Is it the flat four?" "No it has a four cylinder inline water cooled engine." "I do not really want to sell it." "Well why sell it then?" "I have to, I have always been a surfer but I have got big problems with my ears. It is something I picked up from so much sea water when surfing." "Also I have MS." "Well I am sorry." He then told me all the places he had been surfing. Well getting not only a camper but a surf bus was big street cred. Well the camper cannot be that bad, and he had been all over the place. As I asked "Is it rusty underneath?" I realised I should have not said that. "No it is very good for its age." O.k. that's nice. Having a look inside it was not bad, it had a cupboard and also a bed. Well what more could a chap ask for?

"O.K." he said "I will take you for a run." It turned over very slowly then fired up, knock, knock, knock clouds of smoke appeared along the side of the van. "It's nothing" he said "It has not been started for some time." Pooh I thought and away we went. He started to loosen up and chatted a bit. The way he was with the van you could tell he was very fond of it, NO NOT IT BUT HER. I think he loved her.

We went up a long winding hill, she was pulling very well and the smoke had cleared. This can't be that bad. He then pulled into a layby and said "Have a go." "Well O.K." Finding the gears is quite an achievement, there was so much movement on the gear stick, but he talked me through it and I got first gear. "Is that ever right?" "Oh they are all the same, it's the linkage, it has to travel to the gearbox at the back of the van, its normal," "Well o.k." So away we went, now to find second gear. "No" he said "That is the wrong way." He then told me that the gearbox is the opposite of normal cars because the gear box is at the rear and facing the other way. Right now I have that sorted, I try for second gear, (got it). Quite thrilled about this achievement I attempt third. He is guiding me through every move, (good job there is not much traffic about). Finally I shifted into forth gear, great I had made it. He then told me there were five gears. I wondered where that would be Oooohhh Lord, but with instruction I was in fifth gear and pulling hard. To own one of these you must have long arms. I pulled into a layby quite relived to hand it back to him.

My next question was "How much do you want for her? Without hesitation he replied £2,500-00.

My friend had said from what I had told him to spend no more than £2,000.00. I sat there thinking, thoughts were whizzing around in my head. I think it is great but I do not let him see I like it that much. "Well I can give you £2,000-00." There was no hesitation in his reply "NO." "Ooh, I have not got loads of money." "Well I want more than that, it's a good van." Yes it is I think, Ooooh I hate this sales thing. "O.K. my final offer is 2,250.00." "O.K. that's a deal" and he shook my hand. "When can I have it? I told him I could leave a deposit and I handed over the £500-00 in cash. He reached into his pocket and wrote a receipt out for the £500-00.

"I can get a building society cheque on Monday" "O.k. say Monday morning at ten thirty." We shook hands again, I am not quite sure why. He then drove us back to his house, got out, locked the doors and walked to his house leaving me stood on the pavement.

Well with him gone I had a good look around her, (not bad) but Ooooh someone had stuck what looked like an ice cream top on the van. It did look ugly, plus it was white and made of fibre glass. It looked glued on and not a very good job. Oh well I can always cut it off.

I finally left her parked in the road walking backwards up the pavement to my car. I drove home and went happily off for my sleep.

DREAMING OF FREEDOM

After my four hours of quite sweet dreams, blue campers touring all over Europe, sunny beaches and high mountains Ooh what a life!
    I awoke to a bumping about downstairs. It was my Son. I shouted down to him and he appeared with a cup of tea. "How did you get on?" "I bought it" "How much?" "£2,250-00." "Well that not bad, I had a look at it but I was too late, you had already gone." "Well what do you think of her?" "Looks just the job for you", when do you pick it up?" "Next Monday 10.30am after I have been to the building society. "O.k. that's good I will take you over there." "Great."
    I then got up and we went to the local pub, sat and chatted, mostly about my dreams of my new very old camper van of sorts.

PREPERATIONS

Sunday was spent clearing the yard to enable me to park her. My gate is quite narrow so I would have to be very careful when driving in and out.

Monday morning arrived. My son picked me up. I think he was as thrilled as I was. He dropped me off in the town to pick up the cheque. I had brought my passport with me in case there was a problem drawing a large amount of money, well that is a large amount of money for me to draw out.

It was no problem and I skipped out with the cheque. Off we went and we pulled up at 10.30am. The man appeared at the same time, I introduced him to Dave and after very short negotiations we were soon completed (he did seem in rather a hurry). I realised that his hurry was self-preservation, he was finding it hard to part with her. His departing words were as he handed over the keys were "Look after her." "I will" I replied not realising how much I would look after her.

Well there we were stood in the road, Dave said "Are you o.k. to drive her? "No not really, but I am ready to have a go." He said "just follow me, remember it a bit longer than your truck."

O.k. this is it, I turned on the ignition and over went the starter knock, knock, knock as the big diesel fired billowing clouds of smoke. I found first gear, away I went, how far can you go in first gear? Finally I got second gear. There was no going back now I was on the road again. After several missed gears and a few stops I arrived home. Dave said "You are a bit slow." Slow my foot, the gearbox is backwards and there is so much movement you don't know where you are, but I am back and practice makes perfect.

Over the next few weeks I was getting familiar with the workings of it all. The gas cooker that fitted on top of the cupboard. The curtains were total black outs and I still have them today 20 years on. The bed was quite basic, well it was not a bed it was a board with a mattress on it (SO IT'S A BED). I did a lot of cleaning and washing things, it was beginning to feel like mine. I found a camping table in my shed plus a chair so these could be stored in the ice cream top together with my sleeping bag. In fact a lot could be stored in there.

With this ice cream top, he had put the top on then cut a four foot hole in the roof. This allowed access to the top and you could also stand up to cook so it was quite useful but so ugly. I planned at some date to remove this top and fit a popup top.

OUT FOR A DAY

So the plans were coming together for my first sortie, which was to go shopping one morning, do my shopping then find a place to park, sleeeeeep, then drive home. That way I have been out for a day, a complete day.

I selected a town, one that was not too busy. Knowing that area well I knew of some very nice quiet areas that I could park up for a sleep.

The morning came so with a sandwich and a drink stowed away I was off, buzzing along. Oooh it's nice to drive when you have had some practice. I had only been out twice with her, this was my third trip. I finally arrived, o.k. find a car park. Um found one, but she is a bit bigger than the normal car. I finally found a place where I could drive in and straight out. Now to shop, with my dark glasses on I set off. Not that I wanted anything but I was out for the day. I did go into Halfords and bought some rubber mats for my camper. I also went into another shop and bought a rug for the centre part of the camper. My thinking was to warm my feet when getting out of bed. I went into a café and had a cup of tea, depositing myself looking at a wall. I was doing a great deal in one day, so doing my best to conserve my energy by speaking to no one if I could help it.

Back to my camper, I put my new mats down and set off to a more rural area. There looked like some good places to pull in. I tried a couple but decided that they were too near a road, so I moved on again to find a layby that went a little way off the road. I think this will do. By this time I was feeling quite ready for my rest. Sleeping bag and pillow laid out I was ready to sleep. Should I put the curtains up? Maybe not.

I settled down and very soon I was asleep. On waking I had slept for 5 hours. Well, very pleased with my day I packed my things up and set off for home, feeling very pleased with my day's adventure. I was soon tucked up in bed and slept like a log. My new camper works.

FEELING MY FEET

Over the next few months my excursions continued, going a little further afield I sometimes returned after dark. As my cooking was improving I would take a tin of beans or some bacon and have a cook up at lunch time before my sleep.

MY FIRST EXCURSION OUT OF THE COUNTY

Having come this far I was looking to spend a weekend away. My plan was to go to the West coast of Wales but as it happened fait steered me that way. I got news that a dear friend had passed away at his home in South Wales. If I went to the service then I had to make a plan but my thoughts were that I cannot go. After a great deal of thought I decided to go. The loss of my friend made things very much harder, but the plan was made. I would leave home the day before, motor there, find the church and then find a camp site to stay the night. A few days before my adventure, I started to load my things, most of it stored in the ice cream roof. I was carrying food and water so really I had no need to purchase anything while I was away only fuel.

The day arrived bright and sunny. I left home and I had done about three miles when I had to apply the brakes as a car pulled out in front of me. The crash was very loud as all my carefully stored items crashed to the floor. I pulled over and there it all was in a big heap in the middle of the camper. Oh well, carry on. Some two hours later I pulled into a rest area for my sleep. Just to be able to jump in the back, how easy is that? Feeling rested I was away again.

On a dual carriageway nearing Carmarthen I went through a slight storm. Both wipers shot off, never to be seen again. I pulled in and walked back to look for them. I found them but both had been run over so really there was not much left of them. Back in the camper, for some reason she would not start, so in my wisdom as I was on a hill I put her into reverse and rolled back down the carriageway dropping the clutch and she fired up backwards. That was o.k. as there were no cars coming but the smoke from the engine covered the carriageway. I drove away as quickly as I could, then found second gear and was away again. Looking in my mirror I could see cars coming out of the fog Oooh come on get going. At the next petrol station I purchased some new wiper blades. I have since found that any wipers I fit have to have a nylon tie as extra support to stop the wiper turning over. If it turns over it flies off. ODD.

O.k. motor on, sometimes reaching 60 MPH.

HAPPY I FOUND THE CHURCH

I found the church quite easily, then I drove off to find a campsite as near to the village as possible. Within half an hour I was booked into a little campsite and settling down for my dinner, beans and bread but no toast. There was no grill on the cooker and I was not affluent enough to have a toaster. I was into my sleeping bag by 7pm and slept until nine o'clock the next morning.

At 10.30am I was away again, finding the village, I parked up made some tea.

Ooh I need a pee, I did not have a toilet so for now I had a plastic bottle. This will change in time.

My dear friends Chris and Neil. I first met them in Corfu. I had made two very good friends and I think that was the last holiday I took with my wife before she left me. Neil had been a biker all his life. I had spent some fun times with him on the Isle of Man, he did ride a Harley but I forgave him for that. A wonderful man and so much fun. I did not ride with him as he was riding a Harley but I went around with him on the island. He always covered the Harley with a sheet and there it stood for a week until he left for home. We walked into Douglas in the evening and sampled the local bars. We both loved to see the racing and had plenty to chat about.

Because of our biking connection I had taken my old faithful leather jacket to wear at the service. I am glad I did, because there were bikers and bikes there. It was so very sad, and when Chris saw me it was so hard. After the service there was a small reception. I think I managed to stay for a while but my stamina was fading fast, sadly I told Chris "I must go." Another friend said "You can stay in the car park" but I felt in myself that I must go. Making it to my camper I headed back to the same campsite where I settled down and slept until 10am the next day. You could say I had been tired.

Taking my curtains down I realised it was a nice day, so I sat with my side door open and had my cup of tea and my beans with bread.

I was sad and when I see a true Harley rider I always think of Neil.

O.K. LETS GO HOME

Rested about midday I was away heading east. I drove along the A40, stopping for a break near Abergavenny my favourite stop when riding my bike. My camper was running well but uphill you could walk faster (yes a bit gutless). Arriving home in the early evening I just managed to clip the gate post, but I did not look at the damage as I had already hit it twice before. It always seemed to be that sliding door. I will look at it tomorrow it is bed for me.

A LITTLE MORE TO DO

My very sad adventure had taken me to far flung places, I had been to Wales. This had been an improving lesson, also proving the camper was right for me. First the crashing of everything as it descended to the floor of the camper had to be rectified, in the ice-cream roof department. This I achieved by building some slatted doors each side, slatted for lightness. The poor old engine had enough to do without loading it with loads of timber.

After many hours of pains taking effort trying to fit doors to something that was never meant to have doors, I achieved it and to my great surprise it worked, more than well it worked very well.

WHY DO GATE POSTS JUMP OUT AT ME

My association with my gate post continued. I now had a much damaged door. It would latch o.k., but really looked a disaster. I felt that a repair was needed so I took my beloved camper to a local body repair specialist who was also a friend and a TT racer. His first suggestion was that I widen the gate. This I never did but after the cost of the repair I seemed to have become more aware of the said gate post. This was one of the many body repairs I had done over the years. After I had owned her for four years she had a completed body repair and re-spray but as with any older vehicle body repairs are an ongoing thing.

THINKING

After my first adventure I did several trips to Wales, sometimes for long weekends, just getting the feel for my old camper. Many small jobs improved her, really making it easier to set up, to sleep, and to cook my meals.

CAN WE MAKE IT TO DOVER?

As my health improved I began once again to dream (the Continent) Beacons. I think they were very daring thoughts as the engine and gear box were not getting any younger and even smokier. My first sortie was to Dover crossing to Calais, with my large supply of baked beans. This morning I was on my way and she seemed to be going well, distance seemed to make her perform better. I rolled into Dover about an hour early. After chatting to the booking office lady who was very enthusiastic about my camper, telling me how much she would love to have one, asking me what it cost? Was it fast? (No) and about how her friend had one she finally gave me my row number and sent me packing.

Jumping into my camper I fired her up. She grumbled quite a lot, finally starting to cover the area of the dock in blue smoke. It followed me along the Dock finally clearing as I parked up. I hopped in the back and made a cuppa. I had the side door open and within no time I had visitors. "Hello I like your camper." Well that was it, we talked about campers. They told me how much they had loved their T25 but they had moved on and had a newer model. Well we chatted for a bit and as they left I said "what camper have you now?" They pointed "That's ours." My mouth dropped open, thinking that's not a camper it's a bus. It was a very big van, in fact enormous. No more was said as they struggled into their very plush house on wheels. I then convinced myself that they were missing out on not having a T25 (IN YOUR DREAMS.)

I was waved forward, the old girl groaned again but started, I glanced into my mirror and for some reason there was little smoke. I am now thinking I must check the oil when we get to Calais.

The crossing was smooth, it took about an hour and a half. I then sat waiting to drive off the Ferry, keeping my fingers crossed she would start (with little smoke) she did.

LET'S GET MOVING

I was soon on my way, into Belgium, really motoring along. She seemed once again to like the auto route staying at about 60-65 mph. I was enjoying myself, my stamina seemed quite good, and so I motored on out of Belgium and into Holland.

I must get fuel. Stopping at a services after filling up, I sat and rang my friend in Holland who I had emailed many times but had received no reply (odd). There was no reply so I left a message to say I was not too far away and would like to visit. I put my feet up for an hour as I thought and it was two hours later when I awoke. I checked my phone and there was no message, a decision had to be made. Do I just call in to see them or do I motor on? On looking at my map I may cross the border into Germany later this evening, so I decided to motor on. If I get a call I will divert a little North and visit them. I had a look around the shop, and purchased some sort of sausage and half a dozen eggs. This should go great with my beans, also a loaf of very nice looking bread. The call did not come so I motored on. The weather was great, very pleasant driving. It was dusk and I crossed into Germany near Aachen.

TRUST ME A GERMAN DOMESTIC

O.k. time to look for a camping spot. Well within ten minutes I saw what I thought was a car park about 50 yards off the road, but it had big open gates (maybe not), BUT ON INSPECTION OF THE GATES, it seemed that they had not been opened for a long time or closed for years. Also you would need an army of men to close them as two of the hinges had rotted through, so I decided this was home for the night. I parked up facing out with a very nice hedge behind, the perfect toilet. Lord I am spoilt there is a bin to put my rubbish in as well.

I was in the back ready to start my dinner. I had the side door open as the evening was pleasant. My sausage slowly simmering in the pan, beans just bubbling gently, and my egg poised ready to join my sausage, when out of the blue a car raced into the car park, slammed its brakes on and skidded to a halt. I quickly shut my door and peeped out of the window having turned my light off, the cooking stopped. It was a lady in the car and she was on her phone. Well it was all going on in German, I had no idea what was going on but she was to say the least not a happy camper. She was very loudly shouting down the phone and it went on for ten minutes. In the half-light the phone was launched out of the window (well look that's not quite right). Then Ooh no, another car roared into the car park, at this I am thinking this is a bad decision of mine to wild camp, shall I move on? I could because this is scary but it is also interesting at the same time. The car pulled up right in front of the other, in the second car was a man. His door opened pooh Lord what next? He walked to her door put his hand on the door handle and tried to open the door. Not moving it started again the shouting, well not shouting more like he was raving mad. They were really having it to go. I was by now using my own interpretation on the present situation. She was not opening the door. This seemed to anger him because he started kicking her door, and all this time she had kept her engine running. Then there was silence and she started to sob, Ooh I do not know where this is going.

After a little while he calmed down and she finally opened the door. In my opinion that was a wrong move. I was right within a minute it started again, pooh Lord shall I make a brake for it. No too late, he started to get out of her car. As he did so her engine revved up and she swerved to the right throwing him to the ground. Oh lord! She roared towards the gates but had second thoughts as he was still on the ground. Big mistake, she was reversing but as she got nearer he made it to his car. She then took off, with him hot on her tail, as she turned onto the road he hit her with a loud crash. Undeterred she raced away with him in hot pursuit. THAT'S IT, I never did find out the outcome of their little tiff, perhaps I should have found a camp site.

Back to my cooking, my sausage was cold and my beans had stuck to the bottom of the pan as I had not turned the gas off and had left them on simmer. Oh well. I warmed my sausage and with the burnt beans it really was not that bad. The bread was excellent.

I am a happily ever after sort of chap, so I hope they sorted out whatever was bugging them but on reflection it did sound pretty serious.

It was once again quiet. I nervously settled down for the night after using my outside toilet.

I MOTORED ON

I slept in quite late, I think it may have been the stress from last night's antics. I looked out and oh there were quite a few cars parked up. Um I think maybe they park here and get a bus into the town (no idea what town). Well I will think about it. I got my kettle on and once again popped out to my country toilet.

I sat in the morning sun with a nice cup of tea at the same time consulting my map. O.k. the plan was to head to the Black Forest area. This I had done a few years ago on my bike, by taking this route I could visit an old friend.

Well I think I should make a move so after checking the oil on the old girl I was ready to move. O.K. old girl start. She did first time, um strange she seemed very unpredictable. Plus no smoke today. ODD.

I was soon eating up the miles just cruising about 60mph. She seemed comfortable at that, when I glanced in the mirror I could see another T25 bearing down on me. Oh great I wonder if it is an English one. I had slowed dramatically for a long hill, my fellow T25 just went steaming past without a word or a wave. Well that's not fair, what engine has he got in that? I winged and moaned to myself as he disappeared in the distance. That is just not fair as I changed down to first gear and moved over to the slow lane for Lorries.

I soon recovered as I came to the top of the hill and it was downhill for miles after that. Great I let her go, we topped 80mph that morning and only lost one wiper blade. All my bedding ended up on the floor, who cares I achieved 80mph. Who needs a wiper blade anyway the sun is shining. I motored on.

My next stop was for fuel and a wiper blade just in case it rained. There was a very nice services, so after filling her up I wandered around the shop. The car section was very interesting, this is where I got my steering wheel cover. I did not know the size so I was heading out to my camper with two covers when the security man stepped up to me. I understood the word NO, so I tried to explain to him that I just wanted to try them for size. He called his assistant who spoke a little English and they decided I could try them but I must leave them with my credit card. This I did, but one of them came with me to try it onto my steering wheel. Right that one fits. So back into the shop which was a walk of at least 10m. I paid up and retrieved my credit card. I went back out to my surf bus (street cred) it fitted like a glove. From the time I purchased the van the steering wheel had always felt a bit clammy or sticky something was just not right but now how wonderful, maybe I could get another 10mph out of her. I then had a wander around the café, which was nice, very different. They do their own sausages so with sausage for dinner and a very nice sausage roll for lunch I made it back to my little camper. It was very warm so I retrieved my chair from my high top (ice cream van top) and sat with my roll and a cup of tea. I think I dropped off for an hour, well now rested it was time to move on. I fired her up and once again, with a wave to an English couple in a very posh camper I was away. I am finally getting this backwards gear box sorted. Yes the gears are the opposite of everyone else's.

We bussed along covering a good few miles, thinking tonight it will be a camp site. Quite early in the evening I crossed into Luxembourg and started to look for the camping signs. Being a spoilt boy I tried to look for sites near a river or in the very old towns, they seemed to have camp sites where there were medieval type settlements. I wanted just a campsite with toilets and showers, none of the fancy add-ons.

I clocked one or two, with too much going on, shops, bar and games rooms.

AT LAST A FARM SITE

I stopped having a look at my map, I was approaching a much wooded area, and I think this area could be o.k. There is one, it was a small road, almost like a farm track. Well it would be it was a Farm. Great, some sort of stream running through it and just toilets. Hopefully no one will have a domestic tonight. I wondered if they had sorted their problem out or just killed one another.

As I entered the site a lady appeared, very German, a small pleasant lady. Her English was as good as my German (not very good). "Am I in Germany or Luxembourg?" "You are just on the German side but only just." Oh well.

But I managed to understand that I could camp anywhere. Also she could cook me a meal that evening when she was cooking for her Husband (well that could be nice) BUT what about my sausage? Well maybe they could share, I produced the sausage and there seemed to be no problem with that. I think after she had showed me the showers it was agreed that we would eat about eight o'clock. She seemed very pleased to have me camp as there was no one else in the camping field.

I was thinking it would be nice to have some wine so I took off to the nearest shop. That was about five miles back up the road. Good I found it. It was a small super market and after viewing the sausages for a while I left clutching 2 bottles of wine.

Back to the campsite I set up my camp and bed for the night. I filled my water bottles, just for washing and washing my pots and pans.

My drinking water came from the shops. After a nice shower, I took a walk. The land I think belonged to the farm, as the only track across to the wood was from the farm. I had crossed the first field and was just entering the woods when I saw a tractor with a big trailer loaded with timber approaching. I stood to one side. He stopped and with a large smile said "You are staying at my camp site" in very good English. "Yes that's me." Revving up his tractor he shouted "see you in a while." He waved and set off across the field. Well he seems nice.

FRIENDS

I followed the track the tractor had appeared from. I wonder if when he drives the track with his tractor he looks to see how wonderful the scenery is. Maybe not. I walked for half an hour before taking a foot path that seemed to run parallel with the track until I came to a small bridge over a stream. It then forked right, there was a building rather like a log cabin just set back in the trees. There an old gentleman sat outside, he put up his hand so I waved at him. I wondered if I should go over for a chat but it is a bit hard going, him being German and me English so I gave him another wave. I took this route for about ten minutes but I decided I was not going to make it back for dinner if I carried on, so I turned around making my way back to the track. Finally getting back to my camper in good time for dinner. The evening was very warm so I sat with a glass of wine, looking at my map and deciding on my route to my friends tomorrow. Things could change, I hope they do not have a domestic.

JUST A NICE COUPLE

I was on my second glass when the farmer appeared. He introduced himself as Aksle and sat while I poured him a glass of wine. We chatted. I had noticed that there seemed to be very few animals about. He said "My father had built up a large herd of cattle but they had become too much for him as he aged and with me away working in England there was no one to help so he sold the herd." "That is why your English is so good." "Yes I worked in London for three years." "What doing?" I asked thinking it might be something to do with animals or products from animals. "No" he said "I was a bit of a rebel and worked in bars and restaurants." "I then moved to Bath having met a girl who lived there." "We did not stay together for long, I finally met the girl of my dreams who was studying in Bath." "She is now Alina my Wife." "Well I do not live far from Bath I sometimes go there on a Sunday for breakfast." I said "How did she get on her English is not very good." "It is very good but she is not eager to speak in case she makes a mistake." "We chat away in English a lot." "I am sure she will chat to you later" he said with a big smile. "Well how come you don't speak German?" I smiled and said "We are an island and they only taught me Gloucestershire." He frowned, a sort of dialect. "Oh, I am with you." I asked again "Am I in Germany or Luxembourg?" "You are just on the German side of the border." Well O.K. at least I now know where I am.

I said "You seem to have very few animals about." He told me that when he finally decided to come home the farm really was not working very well. His Dad had more or less retired so to bring in some money he had acquired a licence from the local government for cutting wood. Also their own land was carrying many acres of forest, and this proved to be quite a quick turnover of money. The money started to come in. Alina then decided to garden and with his help they developed quite a garden not large, but enormous. They then attended markets and finally started to supply a few shops, so that was their bread and butter. He then said "Come and have a look." We walked to the barn and he jumped on a quad bike. The next thing I was being transported along a track at the back of the house at some speed. Yes you can see why he uses a bike to get around. The gardens were very impressive and very big. After a fast ride around the gardens we went equally as fast back to the house and dinner.

Alina had changed from her working clothes and was cooking in a very nice dress with many colourful flowers on it. I was introduced again and this time she said "It's very nice to meet you" in very good English. I had expected to see some children as there were a few bikes scattered about and other things that implied there were children about but on asking her she told me that both girls were staying with their grandma for a few days. As it was a school holiday and Grandma lived in quite a large town they wanted them to get used to towns, people and shops, as their home was very much in the country.

Dinner was very nice, I think it was lamb. All the vegetables came from the garden, it was very good. I did not tell them I had no taste and smell because I like eating and textures are great, so yes I do enjoy eating and very much enjoyed the meal this evening. I think she was keeping my sausage for breakfast. We did have a glass of wine but they were not big drinkers.

They asked me if I wanted to stay for a couple of days as they had markets to go to and they would like me to come along. Well that seemed like a nice idea so I said, "Yes." As we finished dinner Aksle said "Well I think it is time for bed." "We have to make an early start in the morning." I was happy with this as I am not really a late person. As I left thanking them both for a very enjoyable meal, Aksle said "I will call for you about eight." Well it looks like I am going to the market. O.k. great. I soon settled down and slept like a log.

TODAY I AM A FARMER

I stirred about seven, crawled out and made a cuppa. I completed my ablutions and used their wonderful sit down toilet (the height of luxury). I was now ready to face the day. Aksle appeared bang on eight with the quad and trailer. He explained that Alina had left at first light and had just phoned for more produces. This is how we work if some things are selling well I gather more and take it to the market. The next thing we were flying through the garden stopping at a small barn, loading sacks of potatoes, carrots and some other root vegetable but I had no idea what they were. Then we went back to the house, loaded it into a pickup truck and drove away. It was a warm day so everything looked and felt so nice.

After about five miles we stopped at a small shop and dropped off a few sacks. Aksle thrust a pad in my hand and said "Just ask him to sign that." This I did by going into the shop and thrusting the pad at a lady behind the counter. I could not see a man, she just signed it and we were on our way. (No time to look at the sausages). Well the plan was to be motoring to my friend's but life changes and here I was being a farmer's assistant and feeding people. How wonderful.

The next stop was where Alina had set up her stall. When we arrived she was very busy, the carrots were destined for the stall. These were unloaded and after a quick chat we were once again on our way. Our next stop was a shop in the same town. They took everything we had loaded onto the truck. This done we made it back to the stall and they both concentrated on selling their goods.

I took myself off for a walk around the market. It was most interesting, I found a second hand military type shop. This I found very interesting. I purchased a very nice knife and fork set and a very nice wool hat, not that I needed it as a sun hat, but this would be good for the winter. Nearing lunch time I wandered back to their stall, and to my surprise at the back of the stall was a small BBQ, with something that looked like a very thick oversized sausage. Aksle saw my interest and said "It is lunch." The smoke from the BBQ was wafting over the stall (um the smell must bring the shoppers in) but no one seemed to take any notice. The market almost seemed to stop, well not stop but slow up about lunch time. We sat chatting away tucking into our sausage and salad and the bread was just something else.

They were asking me about my life. I filled in a few details that I think shocked them. I said "I do not really find it easy to talk about, as I am well into recovery." "I just find it best not to not talk about it." While all this was going on Alina was serving just a few Customers. One customer had heard us speaking English, and was engaged in conversation with Alina. She then introduced herself, she was Jenny and she lived in Somerset in the U.K. Well now there were four of us.

WHAT A SMALL WORLD

Briefly she was touring in a small camper. It was her first time on the continent with the camper and she asked me many questions with reference to places to camp. Did I pre-book? "Well no, I never pre-book." "No is that safe?" When I thought about it, yes being a lady makes a difference, so I said "Just keep an eye out for camping signs during the afternoon, then you can always go back if you cannot find a site further on." She asked me "Did I wild camp?" "Yes" was the reply. She said she had tried it and would get very jumpy during the night and did not sleep. I then relayed my experience of the feuding couple, scary to say the least.

I said "Have you a camp site for this evening?" "No." "Well try Alina's it is very nice, quiet with showers and toilet" (JUST ONE WITH A SEAT). At that she chatted to Alina, I think about the campsite as they walked away leaving Aksle in charge of the stall. Well that was fine with him as an hour later we were clearing the stall ready for our departure. The ladies did not come back so after loading the stall and tables onto Alina's van we left. We seemed to be taking another way home, Aksle said "This is such a beautiful country I thought you would like to see this", as he pulled up at a bar. I did explain I could only have one. I had two last night and knew it. He seemed fine with that. I am not sure this diversion was for me as he seemed to know everyone in the bar, plus his Dad was there. ODD. I somehow think this was his regular beer route. This was nice, going into a bar and knowing no one was far different to me, everyone seemed happy to meet me, but I did not have a clue what they were talking about. I just nodded in the right places (I think). I did hear the word spitfire, after a large fly kept buzzing around them. This seemed to amuse them all greatly. A small fly joined in the race around the bar, I pointed to it and said Messerschmitt 109. They found this hilarious and I was at once up graded to friends.

To waves and cheers we left with Aksle's Dad and headed home.

Aksle dropped me off at my camper saying he had to harvest more vegetables ready for the morning. I thanked him for a wonderful day. He said he was delighted to have me helping out. "Do come again." "I will" and away he went.

I made myself a cup of tea and sat outside just thinking about what a lovely day I had had. I was just thinking of dinner when Alina appeared with a big smile. "Did you enjoy your day?" "Yes, just wonderful thank you." Another big smile as she handed me half a dozen eggs and a lump of meat that looked like part of a rather large sausage. "What do I do with it?" "Cook it" was the reply. "How?" "Fry it, it's very nice."

She gave me a hug and a kiss saying "Do come and see us again." "I will" and she was gone. What a delightful couple.

O.k. now for dinner. I soon got the pan on and popped the sausage (OR WHAT EVER IT WAS) in. I opened the egg box and there was a note in there with their address and email. How nice.

Again the evening was warm.

MY NEW FRIEND

With my door open I cooked away, at the same time hearing a very familiar sound. Without looking that was a T25, sticking my head out, yes indeed it was and who was behind the wheel? It was Jenny the lady we met at the market. She waved and then proceeded to drive around the camping field, looking I would say, for the most private corner or maybe the place to be when the sun came up in the morning. She finally settled on the same side of the field, a little nearer the toilets. I was weighing up her camper (well it sounds o.k., in fact it sounded good). I am not sure if it is the same engine as mine. It had a very bad green paint job and lots of plastic flower stickers. Well maybe that is a lady thing, she had not looked like a hippy, and maybe she was a wannabe. Oooh the sausage, just in time, o.k. in with the eggs. No beans for me this evening, living big. Well I did enjoy it. When cooked it looked a bit like offal. I will not ask, not that I would have had any objections to that as I had been brought up on various types of pies and dishes made from offal.

My travels always seem to revolve around food, (well nothing wrong with that). I then wandered over to the toilet as there was a big sink of washing up to do. I had just got my pan, plate, knife and fork in the sink when Jenny appeared. Before I could say anything, she said "What a great site." "Yes it suits me." We chatted away and finally she said "How long are you staying?" I said "I may leave tomorrow." "Oh." "Why have you got a problem?" "Well no, well yes in a way." "O.K. tell me why my tyres keep losing pressure." "I asked Alina and she asked Aksle where the best place was to go and get it fixed." "He told me a place but I am not sure, I don't want to get ripped off." "O.K. are you saying that you would like me to come with you." "YES." "O.k. I can do that."

She then said "Would you like a drink?" "Sorry no, I had a beer on the way back tonight." An enquiring look came back at me. "I really can only take one alcoholic drink in a day at the moment." "Why?" So I briefly explained that it was due to an accident I had had. "O.k. I have some ginger beer, is that any good?" "Yes great." She said "come over when you're ready." I watched her walk away, she was a very tall blond, in fact quite nice.

I finished my dishes and went back to my camper. I had left the door open and yes mossy's were everywhere. At least six, right mossy spray was needed, so closing the doors and windows I gave the van a good blast around holding my breath while doing it. Out of the door with one last blast I quickly shut the door. That should sort them out.

I walked over to Jenny's van, oh yes it was in a bit of a state. I would say it needed a paint job. She greeted me holding out a glass. She really wanted to know why ginger beer, and not beer. I explained more about my accident and how more than one beer can make me a little bit unsociable. She asked if it made me angry. "Well no, not angry just easily made angry." "Oh I see." "Well I don't think you do, I am recovering and it's getting better, in fact I had two glasses of wine the other night and I was O.K.."

"O.k. that's me, what are you doing here?" "I left my Husband three years ago and I took early retirement." "I am trying to fulfil a dream wandering the Continent, just seeing and looking at things and places. "I am doing o.k. but I have run into some sticky situations. "Like what?" "Well men." "Well what about men?" "If I wild camp cars stop to take a look, some drive by blowing their horn, some even stop and come over wanting to chat." "I don't like it, I get scared."

"My advice to you is to stop wild camping" "But I like it." "Yes, but if you get this sort of stuff it is better to be safe than sorry." "Yes but I like my freedom." "Well maybe it would help if you took the flower stickers off you van, they probably think you're a hippy, free love and all that." "What at my age?" "Why not, you are a nice looking lady and your blond hair is not helping." "It is not blond it is grey." "Well you could have fooled me." "Look how long have you been travelling? "Three days." "Your first trip?" "Yes." "O.k. stick to campsites for a bit." "O.k. but I like to sun myself." "Well you can do that on a campsite." "Not the way I do it" she smiled. "O.K. I have done that for years, just leave it until you get to the coast." "There you will not get a problem as loads of people sun themselves with little or nothing on." "Don't try and do it all at once" she burst out laughing. "O.k. I will do as you say." "How long have you been travelling?" "30 years." "O.k. I will take your advice." I relayed a few stories about my adventures on my motor bike. She said "How come you have been travelling for thirty years?" "Well I married very young and I was able to when I was comparatively young. "O.k. got that, can you look at my wheels?" This we did, she had a set of very old aluminium wheels. They oxidise and the seal goes where the tyre seals, causing them to leak. "They will try and sell you a set of new wheels but they can put the thick black gooie stuff on and that will seal them." "Oh great, will you come with me." "Yes." At that she said "I am off to bed" "O.K. see you in the morning."

Back at my camper all was clear, there were no mossy's. I settled down for the night, it was so quiet, so very nice.

CAN I BE OF ANY ASSISTANCE

I awoke to rain, what, rain I don't want this. I put the kettle on, it must be quite early on. Finding my watch I discovered it was 10.30am. Well I wondered if Jenny had gone, a quick look and I saw that there was no movement from that area. Oh good, I had not let the girl down.

She was up and about around 11am. She came over and said "I am ready", so off we went leaving a haze of blue smoke over the camp site. I had a quick look in the back and it looked very cosy and clean. Also it went better than mine. "What engine have you got in it?" She said "They told me it is a flat four." "Well I think it goes very well." It was about 15km to the garage and I think Alina must have phoned them because as we pulled in the chap came out to look at her wheels. Well you could see he was not very impressed, I thought they were crap as well. We followed him into the garage and there were four wheels, which stood waiting for us to look at. With lots of sign language she told him that she did not want new wheels. Having looked at her old ones and now looking at these, I could see these were in far better condition. He beckoned me to his office, writing down 100 Euro. "What per wheel?" "No for four." There's something wrong here but with Jenny's assistance he confirmed that it was 100 Euro for the four. He had had these wheels for a long time gathering dust so she should really take advantage and have these. Jenny was not convinced. I was, "Look that's a good deal and look at the inner rims they are perfect." Jenny asked how much it would cost to change them over. Without hesitation he replied 50 Euro. "Look Jenny go for it that is a very good deal."

After some humming and hawing she said "Yes."

He said "Give me an hour." We walked into the town, the rain had stopped so some people were sat out on the street. She suggested that we could eat, so we found a nice little café down a side street and sat down outside. The lady came out and with difficulty we ordered, two drinks and two meals. I thought I had ordered an omelette type thing and Jenny a sausage type thing.

When they arrived, mine was way out it was more pasta than omelette. Oh well, it looks O.K. Jenny's was bang on. We chatted away, I told her about the route I had planned. She was open to ideas as this was now her fourth day of travelling. She asked questions about camp sites, facilities, rural areas and coastal places. I just explained the way I went about it and hoped it helped. The meal over, there seemed some urgency to get back to the garage. No urgency required, there she was, she stood out because of the crap paint work but the wheels were wonderful. I said "You could have a spray job done on it while you're here." That did not go down too well and she chased me the last 100 Mt to the garage. Well that is a nice job, the proprietor then beckoned us into the garage and pointed to the old wheels. They were as I thought very much pitted, no wonder they kept deflating. I said "I think this is a good move and a good deal." She agreed at last but I could tell she was not convinced. I then wandered outside while she paid the bill.

While this was going on I had a good look around her camper, it was really not bad, it had a bit of rust but just a really good paint job would work wonders. The inside was brilliant and looked very cosy.

"Hey what you are doing in my camper?" "Just looking." "Well not many people get to look in there." "O.k." out I came. She was looking very pleased. Could that mean she was pleased? We fired up and away. We chatted away and she said "Would you let me have your route and maybe we can meet up at another place on route. I had no problem with that. Arriving back at the camp site I got my map and sat with Jenny for a while showing her the route I might take. She was writing the route out, and marking out any of the really nice places I may camp for a few days. We swapped phone numbers and that was about it, she took off towards the house. I decided to make a move, I dropped my 20 Euro camp site fee in the letter box complete with my phone number and email.

MY ADVENTURE WITH MY YOUNG FRIENDS

My camper was packed ready to travel. I fired her up, another groan as she turned over and fired up. Alina, Aksle and Jenny were not about. I was away. I had seen a quite hilly area on my map, about 35k away so I decided to head there. Still in the Black Forest area, it was a great route and we were soon eating up the miles. No need to shop I had the eggs and of course the beans for my dinner. In no time I saw a sign for camping, and this looked great, again a forest trail, a field and a toilet, but what a wonderful setting. I stopped to read the board searching for the English one. O.k. got it, basically find a pitch and camp. There is a toilet but please leave the toilet as you found it. There was a water tap... and boy was it clean when I took a look. It was 6 Euros, not bad. You left your money in this box unless the Caretaker came around. I was not alone, there were about six small tents and one camper van plus mine. I parked up, set my bed up and put my walking boots on. I locked up and headed off along the trail. This is so nice I must walk now. I was thinking how much stronger I was and how much further I could walk. Just half an hour into my walk I came upon a lake, it looked like half a mile long, so I decided to walk around the lake. It was so nice, the fish were jumping. I should have brought my rod. The path was quite well used and it was easy walking. I had rounded the lake and was on the return path when I heard voices. About six people came out from the forest. They did not see me for quite some time as they seemed to be so busy chattering away. Following at a safe distance they suddenly veered towards the lake. The next thing I saw was that three of them had pushed off from the shore in a small boat. As I neared the path they saw me, I went to walk on by when they shouted something. I had to shout back that I was English, back came the reply. "You cannot go that way, there is a deep quarry and a water fall, come with us." They were Dutch but spoke perfect English. "Good job we saw you, it would have been a long walk back." They said "We are here for a week, these are our boats." They were boats but only just, it was some sort of put it together yourself boats but they assured me that there was plenty of room and they were quite safe. We sat chatting on the bank. They were full of their adventure, only one of them had visited this area before, so she was a great guide. She was a little older than the others and they were quite happy to say how old they were and what a great time they were having. They then told me that they were having parties in the evening. This was not the plan when they set out but the chief who had set the camp up with them had disappeared and said "I will be back on Friday" (ODD). Oh well what were they to do but hang on. "What if there was a problem?" All together they said "We have an emergency phone, if we push that she will come running." "How do you know?" "We tested it the first night because we think she has a male friend." "How long did it take for her to arrive?" "20 minutes." "What did you tell her the call was for?" All together. "One of the boys fell in the lake." "Was he wet when she arrived?" "Very, we had drowned him with buckets of water." The youngest one was 17, the oldest one 20, knowing their ages I was more convinced that their take on this was wrong. I think someone was keeping a closer eye on them than they thought.

Well it seemed as I had always known this happy group as they squeezed me into the boat for three, now four people. The other boat was almost across the lake as we pushed off. Well everything seemed to be going well, one on the paddle, just pulling gently across the lake. I just glanced behind me and the boat was so low in the water it was taking water on. I pointed this out to them and for a moment there was panic. Look if we just sit very still then I think we could make it. This was adhered to immediately, there was silence. I did not think that would help but the stillness seemed to go with quiet. No one looked back but our feet seemed to be a bit wet and it was not perspiration. Oooooh shit I am not sure but I think we could be swimming. The first boat was returning fast with just one rower. I did not think somehow this will help but it did, he handed us a small container, which enabled me to start bailing. We were stationary and slowly the water was bailed out. Then holding the two boats together I rolled over into the other boat, pew. Great we set off again and without any more problems we ran into the bank, great we had made it. When everyone got out I thanked them all for the lift. They explained what I would have found if I had walked on. There is a water fall into a quarry, it is possible to get across but you need a rope and also help. It is very slippery. Two of them chimed in saying they had crossed it last year.

Well what a team. We all started back to the camp site, me gleaning more information about them and them about me. As we arrived at the camp site, we said our good nights and they departed chatting about dinner.

THE LATE NIGHT VISITOR

I settled in as it was dusk, I was just making my tea when there was a gentle tap on the door, opening it there was a lady. "Hello, I am Emily, I am with the group you were with this afternoon." "Oh you are the captain." "Yes and I have not got a male friend who I am spending the week with, how they put that together I have no idea." I said "Do come in." She came quickly in and with the door shut, she told me how things were. "They have a schedule of things to do each day." "I go to different places to observe." "It's rather like becoming a scout leader by taking on these different tasks." "They are all very capable." "I am not too sure about the four in the boat but you were not abandoned one of them returned." This was great and showed me I have been fielding a great team. "Well that's great to be part of the team." She smiled. "Would you like to share my dinner? She reluctantly replied "Have you enough?" "Yes loads." We feasted on eggs and beans, with bread and a small glass of wine. We nattered on as we tucked into a wonderful dinner. She was so dedicated to helping young people to lead a responsible life and sample adventure. "Are you in a tent?" "No, I have a small camper not a nice VW like yours, it is old, yes but it's great, I would love one." She said she was parked up on one of the logging trails knowing that they were not scheduled to go that way. She said "I must go, thank you very much for dinner." As the evening was nice I said "Could I walk you back?" "Yes that's fine, we will have to leave quietly", so sliding out of the front door we made it onto the trail. Ten minutes into our walk there was her little camper. I had a quick look, it was very nice, very modern and looked very comfortable. I wished her good night and as I walked away she caught my arm and gave me a very nice kiss and said "Thank you for my nice dinner and your company." "Well that's nice." She said "Here is my email, could you write a short piece on how you met my team?" I said "I do write, so I would be happy to be part of the team." She kissed me again, well this old boy is getting quite a lot of attention. Nice. I trotted back to my little home with a smile on my face.

I NEED BEANS

I awoke to a very quiet campsite, the other camper had gone, and it looked like the pioneers had disappeared once again. I was totally out of bread and eggs, just beans left after entertaining last night, so breakfast was on hold. After a nice cup of tea, I packed up and the van ready for the off. I dropped my two night's campsite fee in the box. O.k. ready to go.

I SHOULD COVER SOME GROUND TODAY

I fired the old girl up, um started fine, but hang on I have a light on. It was the water light and it would not go out. So moving my bed I got the engine cover up and topped the water up. Yes it was quite low, um this was a bit concerning. O.k. cover down, bed back in place, come on old girl and away she went with clouds of smoke. The light had gone out, GREAT. I was away. I decided to head for Alke. While driving out of the forest I was thinking do you really want to go? NO, but there is lots more to see so just get on with it.

I always if possible take a detour around big cities so I dogged Saarbrucken heading then for Strasbourg. I did get on the autoroute for a short while but by this time I was ready for something to eat so I used a motor service. That turned out to be a good move. I found a parking place and went off to the shop and restaurant. Well look at that, ham and chips so after using the toilet, I settled down to ham and chips. The ham was cut from a big ham in front of me. This I tucked into and very much enjoyed, maybe there is life after Heinz beans. O.k. after consulting my map, having eaten and had a sleep, I decided to leave the autoroute and head for some nice looking forest area, what again? Yes I plotted maybe the Malmo tier area. O.k. I fired the old girl up and with little smoke I left my ham and chips area and was on my way. As planned I left the autoroute at the next junction. To be honest the route I had chosen was not the best, a little built up for my taste, you know houses and things. Well do not complain you have had some great country and camping places. I stopped in a small town for fuel and really it was quite nice. Evening was closing in so it was maybe time to find a camp site. No trouble, I saw a sign just after leaving the garage. O.k. follow that, I was just on the outskirts of the town and it sort of directed me back in. O.k. follow it and great it took me to the old part of the town and a camp site in amongst the ruins of castle. Well this looks nice. There was a little office so I parked up and trotted into the office. There was an information sheet on the wall, so after reading that, I bid the man good evening. He replied to me in German so I did a sign job, one finger sideways and one finger vertical did not work very well, as I once found out. I think he swore at me in French. Lesson learnt.

MY CARNET AGAIN

He wanted my passport but I gave him my camping carnet that I had made up myself. I always feel uncomfortable with leaving my passport. This had worked very well and I had originally applied for one, but after a couple of years they stopped producing them, so I copied it from a friend of mine who was very good with a computer and printing, photo's as well. He took it, wrote down the details and gave me a sign to park anywhere. After I had paid thanking him I think, I went off to find a place. There were quite a few tents, but it was a large area so it was easy to find a quiet corner. Just as I moved off (not too much smoke) I had a text message. I stopped, oh it was Jenny. What I read was a bollocking. You left. (True) You did not say goodbye (true). Why? Call yourself a friend. (No). Well the text went on. Finishing very abruptly. Oooh well she let me have it. (I just do not like goodbyes). I then parked up and back to my phone. I texted back I am sorry but I don't like goodbyes. Back came the reply. Well I do. I went quiet.

Setting up my camper continued, this was so different it was really in the town but not in the town, sort of on the edge but the town was just up there. The kettle was on and I went into my cupboard, loads of beans so o.k. there was bread, fine. I bet there is some nice restaurant in the town, um how about eating out, or even go for a walk and look about. After my cuppa, I locked up and strolled up the hill and was soon in the town. At the first bar restaurant they were serving food, slowly walking by I saw, I think a ham type dish come out, um that looks good. I took a seat and the chap came over after delivering his ham dish. I gestured I would like one like that.

He came back, "Would you like a drink with it?" Ooh great, "Yes a small beer, thank you." He picked up the menu and went back inside.

Sitting on the street was so nice, there was just a low buzz of conversation, rather nice. Within ten minutes my ham and beer appeared, on inspection it was roasted I think. I sat with my beer, book, and meal taking my time. Just taking in the evening. That was as far as I went, after my wonderful meal I strolled back to my camper and bed.

Tomorrow I was off to my friend and her bikes.

MY OLD FRIEND

The site was so quiet I slept quite late. Peeping out it was a little over cast but dry. I really was not hungry after that very nice meal last night, and so after a cup of tea I packed up and was ready to leave. Direction Offenburg.

The roads were a little busy but I was quite happy about that as I knew I would soon be in the forest area. When I stopped for fuel and a bite to eat I was well into it. I bought a pack of sandwiches, and just sat with my tea watching the people and the world go by.

I checked my phone and had a text from Jenny all it said was that she was sorry she went off at me. I deleted it.

Before I moved off I checked the oil and water. The water was low again, the oil was down a bit, I topped them up, and once again I was on my way. The old girl was running well but threw up another light, what now? Pulling over, up with the engine cover, the water was low again, so I topped it up again. I had no idea why it was doing it.

On starting the light went out, good. As the evening drew in I was near to Alek. I pulled in and gave her a ring, she answered but was not at home. It was great to hear her voice. We chatted a bit and I told her where I was, about 50 miles away so she gave me directions for the last 10 miles. She said "If I am not back the back door is open." The old girl seemed to pick up speed or maybe it was me driving her with a whip. O.k. ten miles to go following the route she had given me (I may get it right this time) but a mile or two away and oh no the satnav had sent me round in circles, so I pulled over and asked a lady who was walking her dog. Well I did not ask her I pointed to the little village. She went off on one as she did not understand a thing. I shrugged and looked at her and she realised that I could not understand a word. Finally she went onto sign language. To me it seemed like straight on, pointing, then two fingers up (second turning) right, pointing again (straight on) one finger up, then left. I was writing it down, I thanked her in my best West Country accent and I was on my way again.

She was right as I pulled in Alke arrived on her bike. It was great to see her, we had so much to talk about, my trip to Alaska, my accident, her husband's medical and other problems. It was great to see her again, we had enjoyed some wonderful days together biking in this area.

I parked the old girl up and we were soon in having a small glass of wine and chattering away. She said "You can have John's bike, it's a BMW, is that ok." "Ooh yes." "I told him you were coming and he is fine with it." I was not so sure about this. "I have some great routes planned, are you o.k. being out on the bikes after your accident." I said "Yes but maybe make them shorter trips and see how I get on, a good stop for lunch gives me time to recharge." "O.k. great, just tell me if you are feeling tired." "O.K. sounds good." She loves riding and before we have ridden all day with very brief stop overs. We went into the garage to look at my bike and she gave me all the information on her new bike. My bike the BMW was very nice a tourer. "I think it will suit me fine." "Did you do the insurance?" "Yes sorted." "Good."

Back in the house, I went off for a shower. When I came back down there was bike gear spread all around, so after a fitting we settled down to dinner and chatted. She was always a great host. The dinner was great like a hotpot, with a glass of wine. She explained how John was. He had heart problems and had two operations, but he had not been dealing with it very well so he was recuperating under the watchful eye of the medical staff. She told me he was improving and should be home in two weeks if he kept progressing. She said she had promise him we would go and see him on the bikes. She said he was so looking forward to us going to see him. As she spoke about him there was a sadness in her voice, she was not a happy lady and I was not getting the truth. Was I o.k. with that? Yes?

We sat until we both started nodding. O.k. bed. My bed was a very large model, there was not much else in the room apart from this very large vintage bed. She gave me a big hug and a kiss and said "It's great to see you again (AND IN ONE PIECE)." I felt the same. I was wondering why I had been wandering this way instead of just getting here as soon as possible.

As she closed the door she said "No rush in the morning I have the rest of the week off, by the way you know the routine the, toilet is under the bed it's got a handle on it." "O.K. got you, what's the weather forecast?" "Good, go to bed." "O.K."

I managed to get my clothes off just, and fell into bed and I went out like a light.

It was around ten o'clock when I started to move, I was creeping along the dark corridor carrying my Jerimiah, when Alke's door opened and she stepped out also carrying her Jerimiah. Well how we made it to the toilet without spilling the contents I have no idea, we were just in fits of laughter. "Why don't you get a toilet fitted at this end on the house?" The reply was "Why?" We are close friends. What could I say?

The ablutions completed we sat chatting over breakfast. Breakfast consisted of fresh bread and several types of cooked meats plus a little cheese. Very enjoyable it beats (BEANS).

I have your biking gear ready, I borrowed it from my friends. If you remember you borrowed their kit last time you were over. How could I not, I ripped his coat after stopping for a pee. I had hopped over this fence and caught his coat on some wire getting back over. He was fine with it, according to him it looked more used. This was not the way I would have viewed it. Alke brought the clothes in, and yes that's it, but not being content with my contribution to his ageing biker's coat, it seems he had had a go at it himself as there was a matching rip on the other arm, plus quite a few more. Really I found that strange, I would have stitched a small patch over it. Oh well everyone to their own. Alke said "He is a bit strange anyway." Her English had improved so much since I last visited. This made it much easier for this lazy English man.

MANY MEMORIES

Breakfast over and the sun was shining. "Where would you like to ride today?" She replied "Why ask me, you just follow your nose." "O.k. let's get going." My Beemer was parked in the garage looking out, fully fuelled and ready to go. I said "Take it a bit easy." "O.K" came the reply. We were away. Just out of the village and she was disappearing in the distance as always. My thoughts were o.k. go at your own pace, if she turns off she will wait. I settled into the bike, it was nice, comfortable and quite quick. I was getting the feel of the bike and it was good. After about 10 miles on the same road there was no sign of her, so I motored on. The road became very twisty and very enjoyable, in fact it was great countryside. The bike was loving it and so was I. I was now almost turning back on myself, these roads were really twisty. I would say I had done another 10 miles when who should I meet, yes my biking friend, sat on her bike with a big grin on her face. I pulled in and she asked "Well what did you think of that?" "I can say it was quite wonderful." "I think at this rate you will have me back to my old self and I may be able to keep up with you." Her reply was "You poor thing I am just too good for you." I scowled at her. "Just wait and see my girl." There was then helpless laughter.

We rode on, it was just wonderful biking country, stopping about mid-afternoon. This stop I was ready for, we had a cup of what looked nothing like tea but was purchased under the title of tea. We sat in the sun eating sandwiches and chatting. Well I must have been comfortable as it seems I dropped off to sleep. When I awoke you can imagine what was said, apparently I had slept for 2 hours and she ribbed me unmercifully. We got back on the bikes and took the most direct route home.

On arriving home we left the bikes in the garage. I showered then went down for dinner. Alke had cooked a wonderful dinner, and the small talk this evening had turned to me. The questions came in a consistent flow. "You slept 2 hours this afternoon." At dinner and most of the evening we talked about me. How the accident happened and how I had got through the years recovering slowly. She was a true friend.

QUESTIONS, QUESTIONS, QUESTIONS

I gave her all the details I could remember. I did not find this easy but who would.

Some of her questions were "When did you get back on your bike." "When my brain felt it was o.k." "How did it feel?" "O.k. the hardest part was getting my riding gear on." "The riding was just the same as always, after a few miles what unnerved me is that I started singing the songs that I had always sung." "That was when I turned for home, parked my bike, went to bed and slept for many hours."

"You swim now?" "Yes." "How?" "I was taught." "How did you know you would swim again?" "When my brain felt it was o.k. to do so." "Did you want to swim?" "Yes but I was afraid of the rippling of the water, when my brain felt I was ready for it, I started." "Were you afraid then?" "Yes."

"What did you do on the first day you went swimming?" "I changed into my trunks, which was not easy." "Did you swim the first time you went?" "No I was coaxed into the water with two people each side of me." "Then what? "They slowly walked me across the pool then out, I was then taken home where I slept and slept."

"You do work now." "Yes." "Well did that return on its own?" "No, I was taught by a wonderful man in the OT department who unfortunately had the misfortune of riding a Harley, poor sole." "We got on so well because of our common interest in bikes and his total professional and dedication to his job."

"His superior was my own OT, she was also wonderful to me and very professional as is my son, who without him I would not have survived." "I can say all these things now because I understand it, at the time I would question why? what?, what for?, throw tantrums, smash things like plates, they seem to be my favourite because I had no understanding of what was going on at the time.

THERE ARE SOME NICE PEOPLE IN THIS WORLD

In between all this conversation we had moved to a sofa in front of the fire. I had taken a little more wine than I was really allowed. Alke likewise. I glanced up and Alke was sobbing quietly. I reached for her hand and she buried her head into my shoulder and just sobbed. I said "Please don't, I am here with you." "Look what we did today, you ran my ass off on your bike." I said "do not cry it's all good." "I was not far behind you", (dream on) so please do not cry."

She said "Now I understand, now you have explained to me." "You won't" I said. "Why" she asked "Because you have to be there to know, only the person knows and I did not for a long time and neither did other people."

My bed was beckoning me so as it was quite late we turned in.

After a very good night's sleep, I awoke to the rain hammering on my window, so with Jerimiah in hand I made it to the toilet without bumping into Alke. Um, all was quiet so maybe she was sleeping but then I heard her shout from up the stairs "Breakfast." I dashed back to my room, placed my gerry into its allocated place and went downstairs. Oh what a star, she had managed to cook me a sort of English breakfast, no that's wrong it was English with a touch of German influence. She said "Let's have an easy day. "Are you thinking I cannot hack another day chasing you?" "Well I can." "No it's not that, my Company has said I have to go back to work tomorrow." "We will not get up to see John, you will leave and I do not want you to go plus it's raining." "Well how am I supposed to work out what's going on in your head?" "Is there something you're not telling me?" "Yes there is." Lord help us what now?

The conversation stopped when I had a text message from Jenny. It read, where are you? I am near Dijon can we meet up? I miss you. Well what was all that about, she did not miss me a short while ago.

My answer was I am in Germany. I cannot meet up yet as I am staying with a friend. Catch up soon XXX. A message came back, O.K. fine.

Our morning then continued. Alke had the fire going and the damp feeling in the big farm house slowly improved. We both dropped onto the sofa, and again Alki dropped her head on my shoulder. "Look I was not going to tell you this but I think you may have worked it out." "John and I have not been getting on." "He is drinking and smoking far too much." "He is not helping himself, also there are two of us." "What do you mean by there are two of us?" "Well he has a girlfriend." "No!" "Yes." "How long?" "Who is she?" "Where did he meet her?" "Where is she from?" "Hang on a minute" Alke said. So slowly she relayed the ongoing story to me.

"Well John has been off work some time." "I am at work full time." "It seems that he had been going into the town to a bar." "He was very often on the floor when I got home from work, drunk." "It seems that he had met a woman in a bar some months ago." "He has been spending his days at her house and she apparently drops him off before I get home." "One day she had dropped him off, and when I got home he was on the ground outside he could not make it to the door." "I could not wake him up so he ended up in hospital." "I was dealing with this o.k. but I left early from work one day." "I got my bike out and rode up to see him." "To my surprise there was a lady sat with him." "It all unfolded there and then so he is not coming home when he is well enough, he is going to her house."

"Alke why didn't you tell me this before." "I am sorry, I hoped I could keep it from you, but we have been biker mates for so long I began to feel bad about not telling you." "I should think so to." About 2pm she opened a bottle of wine, "Hey you seem to be drinking rather a lot, look I can listen to you without wine being involved." She did not respond with words. She poured one glass each and tipped the rest down the sink.

Well that's a good start. Her feelings poured out again, sobbing on my shoulder. I just listened and she finally started to slow down after an hour. Saying that she had not been sleeping until I arrived and that now she felt comfortable with me. We both fell asleep spread across the sofa. It was dark when I awoke, Alke was still flat out. I eased myself off the sofa. I made up the fire, then went into the larder and found meat, cheese, and bread. I made some tea and took it over by the fire. As I was setting the tray down Alke woke up. "Oh how nice that is", she sat up and we sat quietly eating. She added bits to what she had already told me plus she was worried about the house, she would have to sell it to raise money to pay John off. We talked and talked. She was so much more positive having at last unloaded it onto me.

After she had cleared up she said "Shall we watch a film?" "Oh yes great, in German." "No, no I have a great film in English so that was what we did, curled up in front of the fire, me missing half the film. When I woke Alke was flat out so I gave her a shove and with our Jerimiah's in hand we went to bed.

A LONE BIKER AGAIN

A new day. I awoke to the sun beaming through the open window, No Alke to be seen. I wandered downstairs but all was quiet. There was a card on the kitchen table and a long letter. It read, I so needed you, thank you, thank you. My head is a lot straighter. I have loved having you, please stay one more night?

You can take the bike out, it is going to be a nice day. I have set my satnav for home so turn back when you're ready.

The phone rang but I did not answer it, it would be in German anyway.

Ooh I had planned to head south but no she is a great and true friend, plus I get to ride out all day. Whoopee, I have a bike so that is what I did. Easily persuaded I set off. After a bite to eat at the local café, my bike seemed to get a lot of attention, not because it was English, I think it was recognised. It seemed to me they all knew the owner.

I was away, I had a map but I really did not look at it, I just followed my nose. It was great country, I just went on exploring, minor roads and some tracks. I made it to a saw mill. No one was there so I had a wander around looking at the quite wonderful machinery and the massive trees that they cut up. Back to my bike I sat and took a few pictures. A pickup truck arrived and the driver came straight over to me. I said in a pure West Country accent "I am English, I just stopped to have a look." The reply was "Well I am glad about that, how about a cup of tea? "Oh you are English." "Yes", so we made it to a small hut, which I had already looked at. He stoked up the fire and we sat with a good cup of PG tips. He said "I brought a very large bag of tea bags with me."

Well this is living. He was Dave from Bristol. He was a tree surgeon and had been over in Germany for several weeks, working on some project to do with waste wood. I really have no idea as to what they were doing but it sounded great.

He had worked in and around Bristol, in parks and on private estates. He really knew his onions when it came to trees. (West Country saying). His home was just south of Bristol near the airport. He lived with his mum as his Wife took off with another chap two weeks after they were married. Oh I said "What a bummer that is." He said "Well I did not have time to get really settled." "I now have a nice girl friend who lives just up the road from me." "We may live together sometime soon, but I am scared." "I cannot say I blame you for that." We talked for an hour or more. I told him I was staying with Alke and the bike I was on her near ex husbands. He said that could be a bit tricky." "Yes I found it a bit uncomfortable when I stopped at the local café this morning."

Well the evening was closing in. I really must go. He came across and we swapped emails. I switched the satnav on and it gave me 143km. We shook hands and I said "Keep in touch, I will come and see you when you get back home."

A wave and I was away, the satnav took me on the fastest route. I joined the road within 14km. I let the Beemer have its head, it talked to me all the way back. As I roared whoopee up to the house Alki was outside waiting. "Hey I was beginning to worry about you." "Without your satnav I may not have been back at all tonight." She fell about laughing. "Well it's true." I was pulling off my gear and chatting about how I had met Dave. She said "How do you do it." "I have no idea." I parked my old friend up and she said "I am so glad you stayed." "Oh it was the offer of the bike that decided me." She hit me and laughed at the same time. "Hey that was a wicked punch."

When I walked into the house I think she had been cooking for some time. The table was laid, the candles were burning and the fire was on. "It's a bit warm today for the fire." "Atmosphere" she said. "Well that's nice."

She said "I have run the bath." "I did not know you had a bath." "No because it is in my bedroom" "O.k. thank you." She showed me the bath and disappeared into the kitchen. Well how spoilt am I, very, I had a good soak. I washed my clothes in the bath water, then changed into some clean jeans and wandered down clutching my washing. "What's that?" "What's it look like, it's my washing." "You washed it in the bath didn't you" and all I said was "Traveller." She understood, I once had a girl friend who took me to a very posh hotel and I still came out of the shower with my newly washed pants, socks, and tee shirt, she had no understanding and threw a wobbly. I was a lone traveller and it's a habit, which is not easy to change even if you wanted to and I did not.

EVENING

Our evening was so nice, Alke was so nice and talked more freely about the situation she had found herself in. She asked me what I had planned for the future. I said "I have my life back, I am one of the lucky ones and I have a life." "That is as far as I look at the moment."

We sat, ate, talked and reminisced about the past and also the few days biking we had shared once again. Dinner was some sort of bird dish and very enjoyable, what bird she would not tell me. German most likely, it did once have feathers because I found one, well a bit of one. The starter was some sort of pate. After dinner we cleared up and then retired to the sofa, the loan traveller was kicking in again.

The film went on but as before, I fell asleep just after Alke. We finally retired at midnight.

I awoke to rain hammering at the window, well no biking today. We had talked and agreed if the weather was o.k. I would take myself biking. If not, I would get away moving south again.

SOUTH IT IS
WITH A LITTLE HELP FROM A FRIEND

So after a little breakfast and reading Alke's note, I put my bits into Blue my old camper and was ready to go. I turned the key and she gave a little clicking noise not the usual groan. UM well the battery was flat. Well how did that happen? There was no one around on a day like this, no one was out on their garden. O.k. thinking well the drive is on a slight slope, o.k. I was ready to go, out of gear, hand break off. We did not move. Right give her a shove. Still holding onto the steering wheel I gave her a shove, whey up she's moving. I scrabbled back in hauling on the wheel that gave us a dramatic turn to the right. WRONG WAY, I whipped the wheel back and she crept forward just missing the pavement on the other side of the road. I also just missed the next parked car by very little, but with all this going on she was picking up pace. Maybe I can make it just over the brow then I am away. As she started to go up hill there was a dramatic slowing, I am shouting come on come on, she stopped back wheels uphill front wheels downhill Ooooh shit. I cannot get out because she may go backwards or forwards. So as I sat, I saw a car in the mirror. He stopped behind me and waited 2 seconds then started to blow his horn. I wound down the window and waved him by, thinking he would see my British number plate and see I was in trouble. That was not to be, as he came by he called out very nicely "You fucking wanker", well who told him. Well that's nice he knew a little English.

Well that didn't help, so I sat waiting. Next along came a tractor, well this looked promising. He drew up alongside me, with a great deal of sign language, he understood. He reversed up and I saw him lower the bucket on the tractor. Ooh no my back door it going to get it.

I was watching in my mirror and he indicated to release the hand brake. I did this and very gently he pushed me forward over the brow and I was away. O.k. second gear, I dropped the clutch and she fired up, I was away with a lot of horn blowing and waving out of the window as I roared off down the hill. I could not see him as she seemed to be putting up a smoke screen. At the same time as I was waving goodbye I noticed the interior light was on, that was the problem. Switch it off. I did. Right let's get some charge into this battery. I drove on for about two hours the blue smoke haze was left behind. I had texted Jenny this morning to say I was on the move so I was heading her way or the last place she had camped. I finally had to stop for fuel and I inspected Blue. The farmer's bucket had not damaged her at all and he had given the tow bar a shove. I then noticed some traces of oil around the rear door, well that must be from other vehicles. So very focused I fired her up and was away again. This lasted for about sixty miles when the oil light came on. Well she must be using some oil from the amount of smoke haze she left behind this morning.

RAC ONCE AGAIN

I pulled over and jumped out with my oil can. As I got to the back of the van, ooh shit, there was oil all over the back door. Oooh my brakes went on, having no idea where the oil was coming from I thought pull up the engine cover. After moving all my bedding I managed to lift the cover. Oooh lord it was everywhere. O.K. I stood thinking and looking around at the same time. Just up the road I could see a garage and a Renault sign. Great a garage. Next thing was to ring the RAC. They answered straight away. I gave them my location after a few more questions they asked "If it was drivable?" "Well hardly but I think there is a garage just up the road." "O.k." they said "If you can get there, ring with the name of the garage and we will take it from there." The old girl fired up instantly and I crept to the garage. I rang the RAC giving them my incident number and the name of the garage to them. They immediately said "You are in France." I had told them I was in Germany. "Well o.k. we will ring the garage and get back to you.

Within no time they were back in touch with me. "Go to the garage, they have your number and will look at it for you." I drove the 200m appearing at the garage within minutes of the RAC talking to them. There was quite a look of shock on the Manager's face, THAT WAS QUICK. They waved me in and three mechanics were soon delving into my engine. They indicated to start it up, this I did. There was an immediately stop, stop, stop. At that the Manager also stuck his head into the engine. With difficulty they relayed to me it's a broken oil pipe to the turbo. What it has a turbo? Well a lot of use that is, could it be any more powerful with or without a turbo? Meaning it is quite gutless to be honest.

They then pushed her out to some sort of wash system to clean the engine off before having a second look. On second inspection, yes it is the turbo pipe. I did say in very West Country "TURBO that's a joke."

"We can repair it, can you come back tomorrow?" Not thinking I replied "That is my home parked there with my bed." "Um that is a problem." "How about I sleep in the camper in your yard?" This was achieved in half French, half English plus sign language. "That is if she was parked on that bit of grass then I could sleep there." From what I could gather as long as I was out of their compound they had no objection. So the complete staff pushed me to this nice patch of grass, my home for the night with a rather nice hedge, toilet to the rear. The Manager said "we will get to it first thing in the morning, we open at 9am." With the compound gates closed they all disappeared for the night. My phone had been telling me someone was trying to contact me. Apart from the RAC. I had been too busy to answer. The text messages were from Jenny. Where are you? I had not said I would join her today, as far as I was concerned she was too far away. So I texted her back telling her where I was and also explaining that I had a problem and would not be moving until tomorrow. A text came back, I am only 60 miles from you I will come and help. My reply was no, I will try and catch up with you in the next couple of days.

FEISTY ARRIVES

Right that's that sorted. So locking up the van I wandered into the small town. I found a good supermarket and purchased a rather nice looking meat pie plus a few vegetables. After that I took a look at the river that seemed to go through the centre of the village. There was a great place to park a camper up for the night but I decided that I could not push the old girl that far so with my evening meal I wandered back in the direction of the Garage stopping at a bar for a cuppa. I was sat outside taking in the evening when what should pull up opposite, a green camper with flowers and a flash set of wheels also a women waving. It was Jenny. How could one miss her with those sort of colours? She jumped out, shot across the road and threw her arms around me saying "I was not going to let you face this alone." "Face what?" "Oh you were so good helping me sort out my wheels and tyres." Well she did not say anything as nice as that at the time, in fact I thought she was a bit feisty or in fact quite a bit feisty.

"Look at you, you are on tea again let's have a glass of wine." "Well o.k." She ordered wine, a small jug of white. This was a somewhat different Jenny to the one I had first met not long ago. She said "Alina had told her a bit about my life." Knowing this she seemed to have warmed to me. The next thing she asked was "Shall we eat out?" I then explained that I had my dinner in this bag and had shopped at the supermarket. "O.k. let me cook it and we will eat together." Lord what a change of character, before this meeting I had been looking around for her broom. Having not poured the wine she asked if they would transfer it into a bottle for us to take with us. They did this with no problem.

So I led the way to my camp site. She parked her new set of wheels next to old Blue who was not going far anyway. I could not run away.

I did say "That hedge is mine." Where upon she said "Men are all the same, pee anywhere." "What, are you jealous that you can't? I was beginning to find her rather amusing.

Well she was going to cook, so with a glass of wine in a glass, not a plastic glass, I sat while she cooked. I had moved to sit in her camper but she promptly handed me a folding chair to sit outside. Lord she is weird. I thought I only wanted a quick look to see where she parked her broom. I sat with my wine quite happy but then to my surprise I heard a car approaching. First the front of a police car then the complete thing appeared around the side of the building. Oh lord what now? The car stopped.

Both policemen stepped out and wandered across. I was looking at the thing they had strapped to their belt oh shit. Thinking it is only an oil pipe, first Jenny now the French police what next? With some hand gestures and very fast French I think they were saying "You cannot park here." My mouth opened to try and explain but before I could get a word out this female head came out from her kitchen. In no uncertain terms she told them to go away. I was not quite sure she was doing the right thing as by the look on their faces we could both be locked up quite soon. I said to her "Don't just tell them we are not moving, tell them why." I did get a sympathetic look from one of them. "Tell them why I am here." Finally she did just that. I was now out of my chair pointing to my engine saying problem, problem. Also waving the garage card the Manager had given me. Instantly there were two happy looking policeman. The conversation then totally changed to my tee shirt. Jenny said "They want to know if you have been to the Isle of Man", so I gave her the story of my visits to the Isle of Man races. They then said they would love a tee shirt like mine. I said "Tell them I will swap mine for one of their police shirts." There was a look of dismay on their faces. With a touch to their caps as quickly as they arrived they were gone. That was a bit mean I have about six shirts with me I could have given them one but they had gone.

I immediately turned on Jenny "Why did you do that? "Do what?" "Why didn't you tell them why I am parked here, oh forget it, it's sorted", but she said "I did not like the look of them." "Well that's not true, you did not seen them coming" and so it went on. I gave up and went back to my wine. Soon the dinner was put on the little portable table. We sat safely outside her camper. What a women she is up and down like the Tower Bridge but really she had come to see if she could help, and I was having my dinner cooked for me so do not complain, make the best of it.

Dinner was very slowly eaten, the empty bottle of wine had something to do with it. Jenny then became very mellow and seemed almost tired. I started to clear the table, putting the plates next to her small sink, with no objection from Jenny (ODD). All afternoon her camper had been out of bounds. She washed the few things while I sat and dried them. All tided away we sat and chatted, mostly about her wonderful new wheels and tyres. "When was I getting some?" I did try and explain again that mine are retro wheels original and the best. "Maybe" she said "but they don't look as good as mine." She said "Oh I think I will have another glass of wine." "O.k. I will bid you good night." Then she said "You cannot go yet", and I am thinking of the Tower Bridge again. "Look thank you for a wonderful dinner but I am tired and I need my bed." On that she moved about a metre across the camper and plonked herself next to me saying "Well you could kiss me good night" (was I on foot or horse back)? I obliged and in fact it was very enjoyable as she slowly pushed me back towards her bed. It was wishful thinking, I am thinking the kissing is very enjoyable, I am enjoying it. With that I gave her the best kiss I could administer. I slid around and stood up. "Thank you Jenny for a lovely evening" as I slid her door open. I then got "Is that it?" as I dropped out the door but not being content, she came as well. "I will see you to your camper." "But it is parked two metres from yours." So we had a few minutes lent against my camper practicing kissing and she blurted out "How did you learn that?" "Learn what?" "To kiss like that." I did think where have you been all your life? The kissing continued in a very enjoyable way, when all of a sudden there was a squeal, "Something has bitten my ass", "Well it wasn't me." She leapt away feeling her backside at the same time. I shouted "Would you like me to have a look at it for you." Her door slammed shut. I whispered "Good night" and crawled into my cosy bed.

OIL LINE REPAIRS

I was out of bed about 8am, I made tea and sat with a bread and sardine sandwich, but I must say I was not really hungry as dinner was enough and it had been a very pleasant evening. Breakfast over, I moved my pillows, sleeping bag and bed roll to the front. This would allow them to get to the engine. Just before nine the Manager appeared. I handed him the key and he said "I thinks it will be about 2 hours" and he looked quite shocked to see a very green flowered T25 parked next to me. I said it was just a friend of mine, he seemed quite content with the explanation and wandered off. Still no sign of Jenny so after waiting for an hour I took off for a walk. I found the river and took to the path. To my surprise there were quite a few boats moored with some activity coming from small, medium and large boats. As I walked the day grew warmer so after about an hour I was looking for a drink stop but there did not seem to be a café or bar. After climbing the bank several times to take a look I carried on along the tow path.

MY NEW FRIENDS

I walked passed a boat with a couple who were sat sunning themselves. I think it may have been the Isle Of Man TT shirt that made them speak. "Good morning." "Good morning to you." "I was looking for a café is there one near?" "Yes" was the reply "You just found one." I was welcomed aboard and sat down with a nice cold ginger beer. They introduced themselves as Tony and Ann. They were in their sixty's and had a very nice cruiser. They had retired and decided to travel wherever life took them. I thought that was really nice, they wanted to tell me they had been together for 40 years and were very much in love. "What about you, are you married?" "No divorced, and dumped on many other occasions." They both said in unison "How sad." I said "Yes at the time but you get over it." "Do you?" "I could never get over loosing Tony." I said "Well your life is nicely different, you are in love." "Well were you ever in love?" "Yes I think so but the last one dumped me when I was very ill, I did not even like her." "Well why were you with her?" "Because I had been dumped by the lady I was really in love with." "She had gone to Canada and within a month I had a letter to say stop writing to me, I have found someone else." Ann said with feeling "How horrid." "So the next one was because I was on the rebound and that's all I can say about that."

I then relayed the reason as to why I was walking the river. "Oh" Ann said "You poor boy." "Well it's not that bad." NEXT she said "You must stay to lunch." I said "I really can't the garage said she would be ready in 2 hours." "Oh" Ann said "They always say that" so my place was laid and I sat having a very interesting conversation about their life together and at the same time eating lobster (how could I turn this down)? Tony had run a small engineering business and had been making some sort of safety equipment for boats and for larger ships, it seems he had done quite well and had sold the business two years ago. They both took early retirement. Ann had been a nurse, they had no children and they said it just did not happen.

After a very pleasant lunch and lovely company we swapped emails and mobile numbers and I was once again on my way. Ann shouting "Come and see us any time, you can stay we have four bedrooms."

THE LASS HAS FLOWN

I finally got back to the garage about 3pm to find my camper parked up in the same place but no Jenny, the green flyer had gone. I went into the garage and with a big smile he said it was all o.k. I paid the bill and thanked them all very much, I walked to the camper wondering what had happened to Jenny. I made my bed up, stored my bits and was ready to go. I jumped into the driver's seat and immediately I spotted a note under my wiper. It was from Jenny, it basically said I waited hours for you, and I have better things to do than sit here looking at the hedge you have been peeing in. I had to get going (yesterday she said she was in no hurry) also I was badly bitten last night and you were not interested. (I did offer to have a peep at it).

I sat thinking, oh well, I have no idea what makes her tick but there again she did drive up here to try and help and she did cook my dinner. Oh well I will carry on with my solitary life. Ready to go I noticed a small bag on the passenger side seat and on inspection it was some stick on flowers. Well that's very kind of her but I did not really need stick on flowers but out I get and stick them to the two rear side windows. If I bump into her again at least I would have landed on the right foot.

ON THE MOVE WITH OIL

I fired up the old girl, she groaned a bit slowly turning over, come on, come on. Finally she fired up, I glanced into mirror and there was not much smoke. I was rather glad of that as the garage people had been very good. I did not want to leave them under a smoke screen. I set off heading south after a quick glance at my map. I put a town into my satnav, that's it. I will have a good look at my map this evening. I was driving and thinking shall I go home or head further South? I decided for now to go south and think again tomorrow. I ran into quite a heavy storm but Blue battled through. I think I will drive for 2-3 hours and that will be enough today. Also I was thinking of the oil pipe, since I purchased the T25 I had experienced quite a few problems with her. Thank goodness I am in the RAC they have got me sorted on quite a few occasions. I was with the AA but on purchasing an older vehicle they said they did not cover an older vehicle going to the continent but the RAC will cover you if you are in the Caravan and Camping Club so I joined them. I also find the Camping Club very helpful but the RAC are great. I was doing A roads, which was very nice countryside, so early evening I started looking for a camp site. That appeared within half an hour so I followed the signs. They were very clearly marked, again how lucky I am? I could see I was heading towards the river. Oh boy this is nice, a very large area set in the trees. I read the sign at the gate, there was English writing, it more of less said find a pitch I will see you later. This was nice.

I drove around not disturbing anyone because there was no one to disturb. I did not park too close to the river as the water looked a little low. I was thinking about mosquitoes who on many occasions have made a meal of me.

I parked up on a nice level hard standing. I was thrilled with the level as I would not be sliding back or forward whichever way the slope went when in bed.

One day I will be posh and have these things that big posh campers have, like tapered blocks. They fiddle and fart around with them moving backwards and forwards and with their spirit level until they finally get it right. Then during the night they fall out of bed because end to end it is level but side to side it is not, so there is a crash in the night as they descend to the floor with some haste. Odd that, anyway I am level both ways (I think).

I had been thinking that maybe I should start moving West and home, when I had a text message to say that someone was very interested in buying my house in the UK. This would enable me to travel more. I had made the decision to buy a smaller home with not so much maintenance. My family had also said "It is time we think, that you had a smaller home." This came about as my left side was not as good as my right, not as strong, so later maybe stairs and things like that may become difficult. Well that back fired on them, fortunately for me things slowly improved.

O.k. that's it. Tomorrow I will make for the coast.

PICKLED PIGS TROTTERS

Well dinner this evening was to be in the town. After setting up my bed, I showered it was very hot water with a wonderful sit down toilet. What more could a chap want? I wandered into the town, the first shop I came to was a wonderful charcuterie. They had everything cooked, boiled, pickled, stewed and preserved. Ooh how wonderful. The restaurant idea was totally abandoned, I had 2 wonderfully pickled pigs' trotters with roast potatoes in my bag. Walking back to the camp site, I did stop off to have a beer, at the same time cradling my wonderful evening meal.

Back at my camper, I sat and enjoyed eating my wonderful trotters, now only eating by textures and not taste. I so enjoyed my meal.

Now to my map. My map spread across my bed, I think Bourges, Orleans, Lemans, Alencon, Rouen, then the fast route to Calais and (well the road may be fast but not a T25). I will get away early in the morning. So still quite alone on this site I retired for the night.

CHASING THE HORIZON

MARK CHENEY

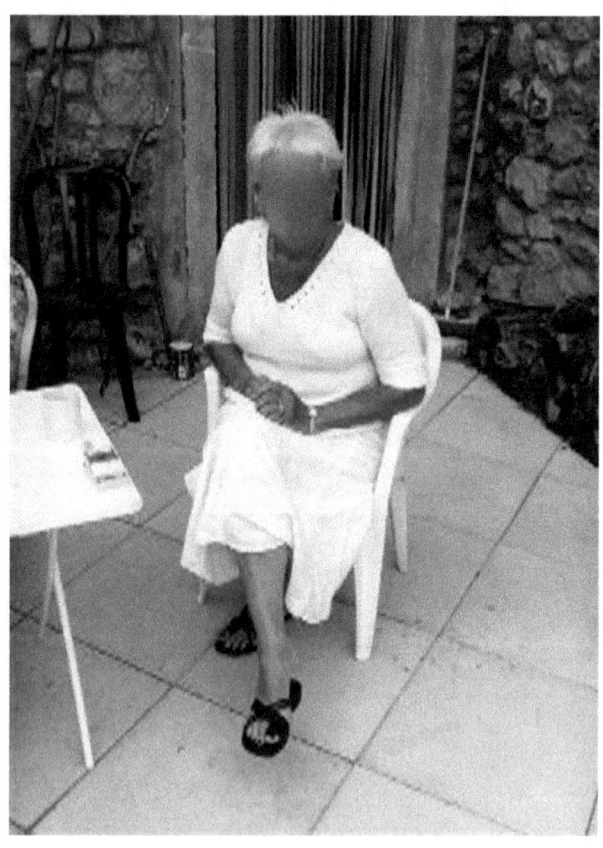

GREAT BRITAN I AM ON MY WAY MAYBE NOT

I was up to a bright sunny morning, but when I sat down outside my camper the urgency seem to drift away, (convincing myself) there is no hurry, just take your time. After a nice shower and the comfort of the sit down toilet I felt I was ready for the day. I sat again with my porridge just taking in the day. I heard the musical sound of a big V twin, from my first observation it's a Ducati, Ooh and it is red. I think it is a good job it is a Duc because the chap looks a bit short in stature, but no it is not a chap it is a girl, well I think it is, there is a pony tail hanging out from the helmet.

I was not quite sure but I was about to find out. Off came the helmet and yes, I had got it right again it was a short girl with long hair and eye shadow. Well you are a bit old fashion with your observations, how do I handle this? She walked up with a receipt pad. Ha got it, she is the site fee lady. I said a hearty "Good morning" and got the same back with a hand shake. "I like your bike" and in very good English the reply was "So do I." Her name was Anne and she was very much an Anne, very feminine, her bike gear did not do her justice, it all looked totally oversized and quite used. I said "Would you like a cup of tea" she then proceeded to roar with laughter. "That is so English." "Well I am English." From then on with two teas we put the world to rights. Anne was a student doing small jobs to make a little money while studying. Her bike was the love of her life, as was mine. I did say "You don't clean it very often." It also had two army type panniers, they had rips in them and looked really shoddy but there was quite a big stuff sac across the rear part of the seat. Her reply was "I know that is deliberate", giving me a broad grin, "No one wants to steal it because it looks used." She told me she had completely sprayed it with some clear protection stuff so when it is time to clean it, if she goes home to her parents then it comes up like new with no corrosion on the bike at all. "Sounds like a good plan." After a little while we were quite relaxed and I said "Your riding gear is not really the best." "The same thing applies, looking like this I don't get others bothering me like men. "OOH are they that bad?" "Yes" she said "If I want them to be." "It seems to me that you are on top of this biking protection scheme." She laughed "I can tell you it works, you were totally confused when I rode up to you." I did own up saying "Yes I was, I really did not know if you were male or female." She just laughed at me saying "That's the way it works."

I am thinking she is a very smart cookie. We chatted away, I was telling her that I had decided to make for home as I had a few commitments. Having said that my early start had become a late start. She said "I wish you were staying tonight as I have my camping gear with me." She said "You could have a ride on my bike." "Oh well, that is worth considering." As always it was nice to chat to a fellow biker. She said "Why you are in a camper?" "Why not a bike?" I gave her a brief explanation as to why I was sometimes a camper driver and sometimes a biker, also you must consider my age. She just laughed. "I like comfort." She then went on to say "I really do love your camper." "Yes, so do I." She had a good look at Blue and said "I would love to get one like it." I said "I love it too but if you want speed and power do not buy one." I said "They are gutless and it is hard work to drive it any distance as you are trying to help her along." I said "The other day a cyclist past me going up a hill." She did not believe me but it was true. "I will do something about it soon, I have read about people who fit different engines to them, some fit Porsche engines to them." "I just feel I have to do something or sell her and that I do not want to do." Her response was "My Dad will buy her." I smiled "Not until I have exhausted all the options." By this time it was near lunch time and I was still on the camp site. Anne said "If I buy dinner this evening would you stay tonight?" "We could have a party." "Look Anne, I would love to stay but I must be away tomorrow morning."

"So you will stay." "Yes." She said "I love your tee shirt." I immediately took it off and handed it to her. She did not hesitate saying "I have a wonderful nighty." "Great, well I have to go to work for two hours in the town." "While I am away you could take my bike for a ride." "What your bike." "Yes, no problem." "Hey Anne you should not do that." "Do what?" "Let a complete stranger ride your bike." "Why not, look I am not a young student, how old do you think I am." Now I knew I had to gauge this right, too old and she will be insulted, so as I am thinking she says "Come on how old?"

I was thinking she is maybe 22 so that is what I came up with. "WRONG I am 31 and I know my own mind." Well I was quite sure of that. At that she removed her gear saying "That should fit you, have fun see you this evening." She walked away in just her jeans and a tee shirt. Her motorcycle boots did not really go with her jeans and tee shirt. She disappeared and I am thinking I have a Ducati just for me. I tried her coat on, well it is a bit tight but O.K. The helmet was fine, the over trousers did not fit at all, so they were put in my camper with her camping bag. I then put my walking boots on and was ready to go. No hang on I need my map, this I stowed away in my pocket. I had left the back door open in case she arrived back before me. I was once again ready to go but I am thinking look should I really do this. I was sat on her bike when she reappeared. "Oh glad you're still here I left my money in my coat. Again I said "Anne look", she stuck her face into mine "Don't say that again, go and have fun, see you later, anyway don't you like my bike?" I said "O.k. see you later." As she walked away she shouted "I phoned my Dad, he is into travel and would love to chat to you is that ok?" "Yes I said" and with great relief she was gone. O.k. I fired up the duc, wow it was great to get away. I went through the town onto the open road. The biker in me was now taking over, the mist had come down and she was having her head and I was letting her. After a few nice bends I was getting the feel of this big twin, I stayed on the A road for an hour before stopping to have a drink. I had great fun and could not really understand why the road was so quiet and why there was not even a policeman in sight. Do not relax, there may be one on the return trip. After purchasing a not very English cup of tea and fuel for the bike, I was on the return run back to the camp site. To say I was loving it was a complete understatement. While enjoying my ride I was very aware of the speed limit. Uncanny I am thinking, as I spotted something that made my right hand shut the throttle with haste. What I believed was up ahead was the French Police Force. I had been on the speed limit so I had no thought of being pulled over but as I approached them I was waved over. I did not want this, nothing was said they just looked at the bike. There were some comments but nothing that I could understand. Then one of them spoke to me, "Sorry I am English." They looked at one another stood back and waved me through. I did not say thank you, I was gone. Whatever they were looking for was not an English man. I rolled into the campsite after about a three hour ride. Anne was already there and did look a little relieved to see me, her tent was up, plus another one, which I presumed belonged to her Dad.

Hey "Did you enjoy my bike." "I loved it." "Good, my Dad has just popped into the town to get a bottle of wine." "What's you Dad wearing?" She said "Shorts and tee shirt, he is quite tall." "I saw him, I though he was going to throw himself into the road trying to catch my attention." "I just thought he was someone who appreciated the sound of a big twin."

On removing my gear that fitted me far better than it fitted Anne, she was saying "My Dad so wants to meet a fellow traveller." "Great how does he travel?" "On his peddle power, his bike?" "Really?" "Yes and he has lots of stories to tell." "O.k. Great what's his name?" I asked before he got back to camp. "Eric." "Is that French?" "Very." "Well it is also English."

By the time Eric arrived Anne was busy in my camper cooking our evening meal. I was formally introduced to her Dad. I had only met his Daughter a few hours ago and their English was very good. I felt a bit bad but did explain once again that at school they only just taught us Gloucestershire.

Well both Eric and Anne turned out to be great characters. Anne was quite an enthusiastic lady, her Dad was the same but very controlled and softly spoken. I do not think there is a country left in Europe that he had not ridden through and his Daughter is heading the same way, a great traveller. She had ridden over the Alps at the end of the summer. This turned out to be quite an adventure, having had lifts in the back of vans to get her bike off the mountains because of deep snow that was not expected and she had found out first thing in the morning that she had to find her bike from under the snow first. I think she will be off around the world in the not too distant future.

All this talk was going on while we ate this wonderful meal cooked by Anne. To date I have no idea what it was, vegetables and a sauce but I had no idea what the meat was. We were too busy chatting about travels for me to even think of asking her.

ALCOHOL

Eric question me on my bike trips also saying that sometimes he had been very scared and had sometimes ran into a few unsavoury characters from whom he had had to made a dash for it. Once he had lost his panniers leaving a group who had stopped him on the road, forcing him to join their camp fire. Drink was their problem, they insisted he stay and after they had taken his panniers off the bike they seemed to gain confidence knowing that was everything he had. He said he was panicking and he had shouted at them after he had tried to explain that he wanted to pee. This was o.k. he got up and walked towards his bike. As he neared his bike a hand came onto his shoulder, so in this position he took his pee. As he turned to walk back he gave his keeper a big push and being so drunk he went sprawling. Eric grabbed his bike and was away, fortunately it was only a short climb to the top of the mountain. He started dropping down the mountain, no one would catch him now. The first town he came to he looked for a Police Station but being late it was closed.

Fortunately he had his money and passport in a money belt. After finding a hotel right in the town, he unloaded his plight onto the Receptionist, who immediately rang the Police with the same result, nothing. They stowed his bike at the rear of the hotel. He sat quietly eating a sandwich the Receptionist had made for him. Before retiring to bed he said that it took some time for his heart to slow up. "What did you do the next morning?" "Well I did nothing" was his reply "The Hotel Manager drove to the place." "All he found was the smouldering ash from the fire and a load of bottles and cans." "That was goodbye to my kit."

All evening we swapped stories, they both said they would buy my books. Eric loved my camper, he had a small camper and he sometimes drove to an area then set off exploring the area on his bike, always knowing that he has a good comfortable bed when he got back. If he was too far way he just got Bed and Breakfast.

We all had a very enjoyable evening. I do not think there will be an early start in the morning.

I settled into my nice bed, Anne and Eric to their little tents. Good fun, good friends and a good night.

CAN I MAKE IT TO RUE

The morning was a little dull and over cast. I made my tea and on looking out saw Anne just starting her bike and she was away. Eric was packing up his tent. I made him a cup of tea, which I do not think he appreciated very much, I think he is a coffee man. He gave me a big hug and said "Keep in touch." We never did.

O.k. I am away, I fired the old lady up and with a long groan she burst into life.

As I drove out of the camp site I thought I did not pay Anne the camp site fee. I stopped and dropped the cash into her tent, then I was away.

We motored on steadily taking the road I had ridden yesterday but at an enforced leisurely pace. I was hoping all being well I could be around Rouen and make it to a small village about 40 miles out of Calais.

RUE

Mid-afternoon, yes I should make it. I have stayed there many times. It is remembered for the wonderful toilet and shower block and the super market just over the road. The town is named Rue. As before there were three overnight parking places vacant. I parked up as the attendant came over. He greeted me with "You return?" "Yes, once again." "Just the one night, Calais in the morning." He was a man of few words but kept the camp site pristine. He also smiled, nice really.

My first job was a good shave and shower, then I went across the road to the super market to buy my dinner. After such a nice meal last night I came back with a pack of sandwiches as I was still stuffed from last night.

I was first directed to this site some years ago. I had driven up through Spain steadily moving north to go home, when just outside of Calais I came upon Rue. I then looked for a camp site and found one, it was a privately run site but to my surprise as I rolled onto the site having looked at the charges on the welcoming board, there were quite a few British camper vans.

I sat for a while trying to work out how much these large campers could be worth. While I did this, Blue was smoking the area a little. I decided to look for a pitch. That looks a nice place so I put my noisy rumbling diesel in reverse and reversed it in between two lovely large campers. As I jumped out to stretch my legs a very nice man appeared in front of me. Boy was he smart in his mole skin shorts, his immaculately ironed shirt, his leather sandals and white socks. "Hello" I said "Nice site, bit expensive." "Yes, very nice site" he replied. "We love to stay here" he said. "Well I think I will stay the night" I said. "There are lots of camp sites around here, there is a very nice municipal just up the road and it is a lot cheaper" he said. I wondered was it my khaki shorts with a tear in the ass, the colourful patches of my quite worn Isle of Man tee shirt, or was it the flowers I inherited from Jenny? Something was telling me they were not very comfortable with my presence. I took directions, why I did that I have no idea. I wished him well and fired up the old girl. I let her tick over a bit, the windows were closing in unison. I slowly moved off giving a wave, not a West Country happy to see you wave, it was a bit more like a royal wave.

It had been nice to meet him, a pompous prick with his head up his own ass. On driving away I was thinking maybe they have a sinister meeting. A get together, what sort of get together? Oh I am glad I got away, I rammed my foot down but she did not respond but just coughed and crept forward. My excuse is she is an old lady and likes to take her time. Oooh it's so frustrating.

That's how I was directed to the municipal campsite in Rue.

I had similar happenings at Calais port, sometimes if I was early for the Ferry or I had decided to stay overnight I would drive into the camper park, I would sit for a short while working out were I would like to park. I would then move forward, park in amongst the posh campers and slowly they would all move. This is true, they would not allow themselves to be humiliated by a vintage camper that had flowers on the windows.

On one occasion I parked and they all moved, apart from one who was determined they were not going to move. I was also getting very evil looks from them so I decided to get out and clean my windows. Was it down to the shorts, my old friends with patches and the small tear in the ass on them? Evil looks were coming my way so in my wisdom I took a leak against my lovely 1988 retro wheels. Before my leak was completed I heard their 6 cylinder diesel purring into life and glide away vacating the area that was now just for me.

Over my years of travelling with both my bike and camper, I have run into many problems mostly mechanical. Many times I have had help from fellow travellers of all nationalities. The British have been great as well but on occasions I have run into a very serious class problem and they won't help you in any way.

Having said that on one of my journeys home I had stopped at a rest area just off the auto route for the night. I had purchased fuel and had been to the shop. I then parked up for the night. In the morning I could not find my wallet. I searched the van and found nothing. I retraced my steps to the garage and shop asking if anyone had handed in a wallet, keeping an eye on the grass I had walked across. I found nothing. I first rang to cancel my credit card and that done I sat thinking I have a tank full of diesel but that's not going to get me home.

So I had a wonderful idea, why not try and sell your books, so with books and cards at the ready I sat in the car park and targeted any English car that looked somewhat normal to me. I saw a couple walking back to their car and I had no doubt they were English. I stopped them by saying "I am sorry to do this but I have lost my wallet and wondered if you would be interested in buying my books." The lady spoke as her Husband fell in line behind her. "What are your books about?" I said "They are traveller's stories, well my life." "How much are they?" "They are 10 Euros each." "Show me." I produced my books and she flicked through the pages and said "What do you think dear." "It is totally up to you my love" he said. Oh for goodness sake make a decision for once, I could see a domestic looming. "O.k. I will take them" turning to her Husband and holding out her hand for the money. Well at least she trusts him with the money. She muttered something about him being too tight for his own good. With money in hand they bid me good luck and were on their way.

I worked out I needed to sell 2 more books and that would get me home. I approached several people, most of them said they were not interested. However, one couple I approached said they did not read books but to just give them a minute. They had a little chat and she came back and handed me 20 Euro and said "We do not want your books but if you send us the money back when you get home we would be happy to do that." Well what can you say? "Great and thank you" so we swapped addresses. She quietly said "We decided to help you because of your tee shirt my Husband is a biker as well." Well what could I say other than "Thank you?" With my 40 Euros I could make it home. On my journey home the last few miles to home I was running on fresh air but made it. My first job was to write a cheque and post it. It was so nice of them. They did email me saying thank you and that they were going to the TT I cannot remember the year but it was like 2 year's time.

Back at Rue I made a cup of tea, had my sandwiches and settled down for the night.

GREAT BRITAN HERE I COME AGAIN I THINK

I was around bright and early, just a cup of tea and away, the old girl gave a very slow response on trying to start but finally she fired up. I motored across country before joining the dual carriageway to Calais Port. Straight onto the port and stepped out at customs. The customs Lady said "I like your camper I am hoping to get one." I said "Make sure it's got a bigger engine in it as these were not made for speed." "Oh" she said "I would not know anything about engines I just love the look of it." "Well so do I." She handed me my parking number. I finally found the parking area, it is not easy there were so many parking areas with high numbers.

    I dived in the back, made a cuppa then sat waiting to be called on to the Ferry. That call came quite soon, up the ramp and parked I then looked for the breakfast area. I tucked into a good English breakfast, then put my feet up in the lounge and slept until the call came to return to your vehicles. Keeping my fingers crossed hoping the old girl would start and reluctantly she did.

HOME

I was away but as always with the old camper and flower power the customs pulled me in yet again. We went through the usual where have you been? Open up the side door. All O.K. and on your way.

Out of the port I got a move on but after a short while you have to climb out of Dover so I tootled up the hill with everything flying past me. When it levelled out I was able to keep up a steady 60mph. Then onto the M4 and home, we made it once again. I did get a text message from Jenny, just to say hope you had a good trip.

I text her back, Home and safe.

LIFE FORTUNATELY GOES ON

I finally moved house and settled in as best one can. My bikes tucked away in the garage. Blue not fairing so well. Parking was a problem so a friend of long standing offered to park her up at his house. I was busy with insulating the house and making it comfortable, so this arrangement suited me well. Also with riding my bike I was beginning to stretch my legs staying out for longer periods and sometimes riding with my friend Tabitha. I was finding that I was beginning to like company, before I had always been a lone traveller.

TOURING ALONG THE MOUNTAINS

A friend and I did have a week away riding with a couple who I thought were harden travellers but finding out as you do they were nothing of the kind.

The trip was along the French Pyrenees. We camped more than stayed in accommodation. The route was very nice and the weather was mixed but getting a little cold in the evenings.

My philosophy when travelling is always be prepared, but there was none of that. I would say o.k. shop in the morning make sure you have food for the evening but this never happened. Towards the end of the day there was a big rush and tear to find a campsite plus food. They were a very fiery couple and there was always an exchange of words (i.e. a domestic) every morning and evening. Plus he seemed to get pleasure in revving the balls out of his bike while they were having words about packing the bike. This would happen in the morning. Any words of advice seemed to evaporate into the air. Their performance began to amuse us and it became so predictable. It seems normal for them. I gauged it to be rather like Vesuvius, it would erupt in seconds and would burn out as quickly as it started. During the day the riding was great so if there was confrontation we did not witness it but when we did at times it was not nice. I think some temper control should be advised. On nice days we would stop quite a lot and take in the wonderful country we were riding through. Many of the rivers were very low, in fact some of them had totally dried up.

I believe they divorced some time later. Sad I feel it does not take much to be a little considerate on both sides, but who am I to talk, I have divorced and parted on a few occasions.

WOULD YOU LIKE YOUR CAMPER BACK

Back to my camper old Blue, she had been with my friend for some while, I said to him one day "If you would like to use her it is fine by me." Well this became a learning curve.

In fact after some trips he found he very much enjoyed the camper and we agreed a price that he would pay me for her. How could I sell the love of my life my Blue?

This was supposed to happen but over a period of time no money transpired. It did not seem to bother me as I was using my car. That was quite powerful and would cruise all day at a good speed. I had a small tent that you attached to the back. It was a great idea and I enjoyed my time travelling with it, but the only problem was you could not just pull over and stay the night, so in that sense I was missing my camper. I began to think as I had received no money from my friend, I wonder if I could get the old girl back. Before I could ask the question I had a phone call saying would you like your camper back? YES I WOULD.

BLUE COME HOME I AM SORRY
MODIFICATIONS AND TESTING

Arrangements were made to collect my lady. On the day I arrived I was feeling quite thrilled about having her back also feeling sorry that I had abandoned her. My plan was to cut the ice cream top off and fix a pop up roof over the cooking area. There she stood looking quite good but on opening the doors my mouth dropped, no curtains, no covers on the sleeping foam mattresses, she looked used. Also there was a table stand in the middle of the floor. The radio was just taped to the dash. I spoke to my friend later saying "You did not cut into the steel chassis did you?" "Oh no, I didn't" but oh yes he had and it looked to me that he had cut it with a hammer and chisel. I was shocked to also find out that a water hose had broken and he had driven half way up Porlock with no water in the engine. Lord this is not sounding good but starting with the roof in mind I proceeded with the job in hand, cutting the roof off with a small disc cutter and riveting some aluminium plate to the top to reduce the hole size. With a piece of ply to cover the hole I was ready to take her home.

She burst into life and sat loudly knocking away. She drove about the same, slow and without much energy, the low water light came on before I arrived home. I went to work cleaning her from top to bottom and with my old friend Maurice a pop up top was designed and fitted. It was a great job and all credit to Maurice. How we can work together I have no idea, it is a laugh from start to finish.

He was with me when I decided to replace the wood liner on the floor. This is when we found this enormous hole cut into the metal chassis of the van. A patch was made and moulded in before the wood was replaced. We were not pleased at the way the hole had been cut but out of site out of mind.

OLD BLUE GAVE UP

On my next run out after topping up the water she seemed o.k. but after a few miles the low water light came on again. She went into the garage but they found no leaks so I convinced my Son to take her away for a week. He was thrilled but on the morning of his departure I had a phone call from him, he was on the M4 and old Blue had given up. She was already on the break down truck on her way back. By the time he arrived back I had my car loaded with all its gear and the tent that fixes to the back of it. He was soon away and made the port just three hours late. Off to France he went reporting back he said "I love the accommodation."

Blue was taken to my local garage. They were too busy so Blue was taken to another local garage who straight away tested the engine. She was finished. The garage proprietor said he had never seen an engine that had at some time been so over heated.

A NEW ENGINE

It was decided to have a recondition engine. This was down to me to find a suitable engine supplier. I found a Company through a camping magazine. The price was around £1,000.00 together with exchanging my engine. After long chats with the proprietor, he had convinced me this was the right way to go. I paid the money and we waited for the engine delivery. When it arrived the garage proprietor rang me saying "I think you had better come and have a look at what has arrived." It was a shock when I saw it, it stood on a wooden pallet. It was dirty, black oil dripping from it and on inspection it was far from reconditioned, it looked as it had been taken out of another camper, dropped on the pallet and sent to me. This was not a good situation. I rang the Company and described the state of the engine. His reply was "I have used these suppliers for many years and I trust them implicitly." I said "I will send the engine back to you and I want my money back." His reply was "You have no chance." Now this is not a good situation to be in. The garage is saying it is not a recondition engine and he is saying it is, but to be honest a person without knowledge of engines, to me it looked like it was something that you would give to a scrap merchant. The supplier also said "If there is a problem with the reconditioned engine then it is your garage that has damaged it." My reply was "The engine came on a pallet and it has not moved, it has stood as it was delivered."

IT'S NOT WHAT YOU KNOW
IT'S WHO YOU KNOW

The messages went on for 2 weeks but he was having none of it. I had just lost a thousand pounds that I could ill afford.

One afternoon I was relaying my sad story to a friend who is also a computer boffin. He said "Give me his name and the area he runs his business from." Later that day I emailed the details to him. He came back to me in no time with the supplier's home address, his home phone number and he had also found out that he was a local Conservative Councillor. My friend also sent me the Council's email address. "How did you find this out?" "His reply was "I have my ways."

I immediately sent him an email asking again for my money back. I also left a message on his home phone.

In no time at all I had a text message saying that you are not getting your money back and do not ring my home number again.

I texted back that I am sorry that you feel able to mislead and cheat people out of their money but as you are a local Conservative Councillor my next message is going to the Council complete with the last text message you sent me.

15 minutes later I received a text message from him, which read I have spoken to my engine supplier and on this one occasion he has agreed to have the engine back. I will also refund your money. What can I say? The engine was returned and after a few phone calls over the next 2 weeks the money was finally paid back into my account!

JUST KAMPERS

The second replacement engine was purchased from a reputable company Just Kampers, it arrived looking pristine, and indeed it looked like a new engine. Within two weeks the engine was fitted and most of the work was done by a very young man under the supervision of the head mechanic. He did a good job as far as I could tell, looking at it from a none professional point of view. Every now and then I bump into the lad, well not a lad now, only a few weeks ago I saw him at the local Pub. We chatted about engines and I then revealed to him that I had now fitted a third engine. With this he was quite intrigued.

Once again I was on the road. I had not found my encounter with this first engine supplier one that I would want to encounter again. I had always known that these people exist but had never had any dealings with them. I sincerely hope I never do again.

OFF TO FRANCE

After driving her around for a week I decided to head for the continent. This I did and I was loving my camper once again. I did this trip with only two problems. In Spain the pressure on the clutch pedal seemed to be getting less. On having a conversation with a friend by phone I thought I could fix this. It was the clutch fluid that had become low. The fluid tank is right up by the steering wheel, the bleed screw is right back by the engine, so it was a two handed job. I then secured a local man by pointing out the problem. He seemed to know what I was asking him to do, he was on the clutch pedal and I was on the bleed screw with a lot of stop, hold it down, let it up, how I have no idea but we did it and once again I had a clutch.

PROBLEMS IN THE MOUNTAINS

The second incident was. I went into the Pyrenees for a day's skiing. The old girl was very good on the mountain roads, low revving so she just tickled up the mountain. I skied all afternoon but on returning to my camper she would not start, she was turning over O.K. but would not fire up. Once again I rang the RAC. Well what a service within half an hour a four wheel truck arrived with two of the oiliest French men I had ever seen. Their overalls were shiny with oil and looked like they had never seen a washing machine. They went straight to the work, the engine cover up, one on the starter, the other one whipped off the air filter and stuffed an aerosol into the intake. She was turning over slowly one or two tired, then the lot fired into life. They said "It is your glow plugs, this is our card we will replace them in the morning." "Pick it up after 10am." They leapt into their vehicles and were off. Fortunate I was with some friends and Dave my son. I was able to get a lift back to the house and back to retrieve my camper in the morning. When I arrived at the garage in the morning there she was sat waiting for me. I was greeted nicely and given the bill. I paid up and was on my way. Beat that for service (I did leave a tip hoping it would go towards some washing powder to wash the overalls) or even a new pair of not so oily boots.

I did several trips with my new engine. I was very pleased with it but there was still this thing nagging at me, it is too slow, it is not powerful enough. It did put up a few electrical problems, pipes breaking, just things but I seemed to be able to get repairs done in whatever country I was in.

While this was all going on I managed to meet up with Jenny once again but on this occasion she was heading home so it was just a meeting one day and then away. She seemed in good form and was looking good, her hair was now a very nice blond and she looked tanned and well.

SPAIN ONCE AGAIN

I in the meantime was spending a few weeks in Spain. The weather was great and I was enjoying the Costa Brava very much. I was camped at Le Fosca a very pretty area. My Son and his Wife were also there staying in one of the hotels right on the coast. After a very nice day on the beach I wandered back to my camper. I went to unlock the door but it was already open. Whoever they were had cleaned me out. They took my computer and also my food. My clothes, my chargers and anything else they could find. After I had a good look through my camper I took myself off to the police station. Before I go any further this was a total waste of time so if you are in Spain and have a problem do not go to the Police. They are really not interested.

In the station there was another chap who had his car broken into at the same place. Also a young couple who were very upset, it turned out that this was their first holiday together as a couple and all their camera equipment had been stolen. Fortunately for me their English was very good, my Spanish was no good at all. We were there for two hours. Fortunately as I did not speak Spanish the young couple were allowed into the interview room with me. We gave the duty officer all our details and finally was given an incident number. This would then enable us to claim from our insurance. That is a laugh for a start, my biggest concern was for the young couple who had today just driven up from Barcelona. They were saying they wanted to go back home. I said "Look you are both o.k., stuff is stuff you are more important." "Please take your holiday and have fun." I think I had convinced them to carry on but I never heard from them again so I really do not know what they did. The next day I was up bright and early, my camper felt dirty having had some thieving ass hole rummaging through my things. I started washing my bed clothes, sleeping bag and even the one towel they had left me. This was progressing well until I decided to wash the small mat that sat just inside the door. Well I shoved it into the machine with no problem. An hour later I went to check on the machine and all was done.

I HAVE JUST WASHED AN ALIEN

I should not have washed this mat. It had blown up like a very large balloon. WHY I have no idea. I had a big problem, in fact it was so big it would not come out through the door of the washing machine, what have I got here? I am looking over my shoulder, if the camp site lady appears I am done for. I have no idea why it did this but I found that it would not come out through the door. I grabbed a knife from my camper and started to cut the balloon up slowly I was pulling bits out, finally what was left with some effort came out through the door. It was so heavy I had a job to lift it. There was a skip on the site not far from the washing machine and I lugged it over and dropped it into the skip with a sigh of relief.

The next day I walked by the washing machine area, there was a notice on my machine, it must have read out of order.

MY INSURANCE COMPANY OR NOT

I then contacted my insurance company with all the details plus the incident number. Some weeks later I had a reply it read. You are not covered for any of the items that were stolen. My first reaction was you are having a laugh, but now on speaking to them on the phone it was categorically you are more or less get stuffed. What I was covered for I still have no idea. On making enquires with other insurance companies they said "You are not covered for the contents of a camper." "What about my computer?" "Why didn't you put your computer in your safe?" "What safe?" So that is it, why do we pay insurance? One big plus was that 2 days prior to the break in I had down loaded my story I had been writing onto a memory stick.

After a few days I seemed to settle again but I made the decision not to take my camper to any more beaches instead I would walk to them and that is what I did.

I DRIVE NORTH

After a great few weeks I decided to make for home. All was now stowed away and I started moving north. I crossed the border and motored up through France. The old girl was slow as always but we maintained a steady 55 mph until I came to a hill. Then it was onto the lorry lane and trying to keep in front of them. Near Brive I pulled in for fuel. After paying I was walking back to my camper and that was when I noticed the rear was covered in black oil. I knew what the problem was so I pulled over to a safe area, thinking I have just about had enough of this. Engine cover up, yes there it was the low pressure pipe from the turbo had broken. I can fix this. After trying for an hour without the right tools, covered in black oil I had to ring the RAC.

The rescue truck arrived within half an hour, the man was very French, but we communicated quite well, myself covered in black oil and pointing to the pipe in question. Old Blue was soon on the back of the truck heading for Brive. In no time at all we pulled into a Garage and my camper was unloaded. The Chief arrived and I explained as best I could, also pointing to the broken oil pipe. He said he would have a good look at it tomorrow because they were closing up for the day. I said "Well o.k. but where do I stay?" He said "camping" and pointed to the back yard where we were standing.

Within ten minutes I saw the last person leave. It was getting dark by now and I really I did not feel too happy about the whole situation but I was stuck with it so I just had to make the best of a bad job. First I found a good hedge to urinate, it was quite a nice hedge in a quiet corner of the yard. This done I put the kettle on and put the always reliable beans on the cooker. I did have plenty of light as one of the mechanics had dropped an electric lead out of one of the back doors before leaving. This gave me heating as well if I needed it.

With dinner over I sat and read my book for an hour before turning in for the night. The yard became eerie, odd strange noises. I was not happy about this but I tried to look on the bright side and sleep, this I achieved.

In the morning I looked out onto a few old scrap cars, oil slicks and not much else.

NO HURRY

I sat with my cup of tea waiting for the work force to arrive. This happened in dribs and drabs, finally about 10am I went looking for the Chief. I was informed that it was his day off, but about 11am a mechanic did come to have a look and returned an hour later saying that it would be a week before they could get a new pipe. It is only a pipe to make up but no, it had to be a replacement pipe. While all this was going I was talking to the RAC. I had explained about making a pipe but the garage were adamant, if they made up a pipe, and it broke then the RAC would come back on them so a new pipe it had to be. The time period to acquire a pipe had now extended to 10 days meaning I had to go home and return when it was fixed.

I HIRED A ROCKET SHIP

It was arranged that a taxi would pick me up at the garage and take me to a car hire company. I would then drive home, dropping the car off at Calais and picking another up at Dover to take me to my home. How I was to get back to Brive I had no idea. I took my small travel bag, thanked the man in the office and jumped into the taxi. I was taken to the car hire company and within half an hour I was in my VW Gulf driving north. My stop for the night was near Orleans. I managed to get into an F1 Hotel, very basic but also very cheap and clean.

I left quite early the next morning and was rolling into Calais in the afternoon. I spoke to the ticket office explaining what had happened and for £10.00 they changed my ticket. They hurried me out as the Ferry was just boarding. I left my posh Gulf parked up on the dock. The plan was to collect another car at Dover. I found a somewhat comfortable seat and slept. This stood me in good stead to drive home. Arriving at Dover as a foot passenger I made my way to the taxi rank. I jumped into a taxi and asked to go to the car hire company. "Oh I know where that is I go there all the time." Well that was reassuring.

MY SECOND ROCKET SHIP

I then picked up my nearly new golf with only 500 miles on the clock. Well what a treat. I arrived home in the early evening having quite a few more horses under the bonnet. I was amazed as when it was put into top gear it would just pull in an effortless way that I had not experienced. I was quite sad to take it back the next day, but this car had given me an insight into modern cars and got me thinking even more as to my camper or not my camper.

HOME

I settled down to life at home and my writing.

OOH ON THE MOVE AGAIN

After 8 days the RAC rang and said "Your camper is fixed, they managed to find a new pipe in Switzerland." "Oh good, how do I get back to Brive?" Well the RAC were first class. Firstly I had a taxi to London City Airport. I caught a flight to Brive flying with Air France. Well when you have been flying Ryan Air and Easy Jet, Air France was upper class, even the seats were comfortable and the service excellent and the meal was very nice. It was also in the price. On landing at Brive there was a taxi waiting to take me to the garage. Do not ever say that the RAC will not look after you, they do.

As we pulled up there was old Blue standing waiting for me. Thanking the taxi driver I went into the garage, settled my bill and after an inspection of the new oil pipe I was on my way. My decision was to give Blue a good hammering and drive straight to Calais. The idea was good but the execution was not. I was soon on the auto route but I had no chance, whatever gear I was in, whatever way I drove, slowly was the speed and effort on my part was everything. I had no choice but to stop for the night. The site I found was saying open but there was no one around so I just parked up had a bite to eat and settled down for the night. In the morning I was ready at first light, I put some money in an envelope and dropped it in the letter box on the side. She fired up and we were away.

I soldiered on making it to Calais that afternoon. Onto the port I hopped out with my passport. Oh not again, the customs chap said "I love your camper." I said "So do I but it is gutless." "Oh but I love it, do you want to sell it?" I was sorely tempted. "If ever you want to sell it let me know please."

He gave me his card. "O.k. I will." Finally he said "On your way." I had lunch on the boat and sat thinking you do so love your camper do not sell it, do something about it. I had once again been reading about people who had fitted different engines to their T25's, just look at it and see what you can find out.

THE LAST STRAW

How wise was this, I had booked a Ferry to the Isle of Man for the Manx races with a friend but unfortunately she was unable to come. I offered the ticket to my friend Dean a very keen motor cyclist. He had just moved house but was very keen to come. It was agreed that we would take a two bike trailer hooked to the rear end of Blue. The idea seemed fine until the morning we were leaving. I met Dean and his Wife at a services on the M5. His bike was already in the trailer, so I thought I was just picking up Dean and his little suit case. To my surprise, no I was picking up his three very, very large suit cases. My mouth dropped open saying "We are only going for a week with a tent and a little camper." His Wife said "He always does this." So with reluctance these enormous suit cases were loaded taking up the complete sleeping area of the camper plus without a doubt this was going to cut the speed down dramatically. With our good byes said to Tash we chugged away on to the M5. Well the journey was uneventful just fuel and oil as the old girl was blowing a little smoke because my foot was flat on the floor all the time. On one slight gradient we were clocking 30 mph with Dean in a flat panic. Saying "Open up." My reply was "Open up what?" We went on without getting arrested or a fine for being a mobile hazard to Haysham. After booking in we were waved forward, waiting at the bottom of the ramp ready to go onto the boat. I was trying not to show the complete panic I was in to Dean. Thinking will it make it up there? The hand went up pointing GO. The panic told me low gear and forward. I shouted to the seaman "I will wait for the ramp to clear." His reply was "No keep moving." I did not, the last car had just cleared the ramp and I sprang forward with a chug. We were going fine but as we neared the top the last car had not moved and was just parked about 4 meters onto the deck. I just kept going until a loud shout came from Dean "STOP" as I gave the car a little nudge. No one got out the car they just laughed well it was a bit of a wreck. We had the camper level and the trailer still on the ramp. NOT LOOKING GOOD.

Finally we were waved forward, with a big rev up and loads of smoke from the engine and the clutch we made it. It did not end there. The seaman came and said "Drive in there then reverse into there." Reverse I have trouble driving her forward leave alone reversing her. At that Dean said "I can do it" so quickly we changed seats and he popped it just where they wanted us to go. How smart is that? We made it.

Unloading and getting to the campsite was no problem. We then settled down to the weeks racing, riding our bikes all over the island.

One day we decided to take the camper. I asked Dean if he would like to drive. This went very well until we were dropping down into Laxey and to me we seemed to be going a little too fast. I said "I think you should change down." The reply was "Well we have brakes as well. When he applied them, the cry went up "They don't work." In the panic I shouted "Pump them." Then slowly we came to a halt. Dean then announced that I really needed to do something about it. Well it passed the MOT. That statement did not help so I drove back.

The time came for us to leave. I loaded the three large suit cases and away we went. Loading at the port went a little easier.

At Hasham we were soon away but joining the M6 unbeknown to me, a strong head wind was developing but with true grit we soldiered on. On quite a few occasions we went down to 20 mph on the M5. How we did not get arrested I have no idea. We survived but I am not quite sure how.

We made it to Deans home, unloaded the three large heavy suit cases and I was away, noticing immediately the power increase. My mind was made up, it has got to be a new engine.

WELL ITS LOOKING LIKE A TDI

On settling back at home in between my writing I was searching the internet and surprisingly there were quite a few people fitting different engines and gearboxes to the T25's. I also went to a local mechanic but as he was just closing his business for good there really was not much point in discussing this with him. Some months previous to this I had met a local garage owner, when selling my books at a small country fair. In fact, he bought a book and also seemed very enthusiast about the bike I had brought with me. We went into bike talk for a few minutes. When I found the garage I had been using was no more, which was when I contacted Martin and his wife Sharon who was not only a house wife but part time garage worker. On finding their work shop I explained what I was intending doing. He seemed quite knowable about grafting engines into places they were not meant to go. This was a great help to me. On the internet again I found one quite local to me, so I made arrangements to visit the following week.

NOT FOR ME

Taking Blue I finally found this factory unit on an industrial estate. Firstly I found the proprietor with his head in the engine of a camper. He seemed a very hands on sort of chap and after looking at my camper he said "I can fit you a TDI with an Audi upside down gear box." I said "Are your engines and gearboxes reconditioned?" "Oh no" he said "These TDI's are indestructible, I just take them out of cars and adapt them to fit." "What about the gear boxes" I asked. "Audi gear boxes are indestructible, no I just take them out and adapt them to fit." As I left I said "I will think about it." "Oooh" he said "Do not wait too long, I have quite a waiting list." This I was not convinced about.

AT LAST I FOUND MARIO

My second contact was a small firm in Telford. MV Engineering. On looking at their website it grabbed my interest, it seemed to be everything I was looking for, I hope.

Arrangement were made to visit their unit near Telford. I spoke to Mario who at first gave me the impression that he did not want to speak to you anyway. I have since found out that he is always so busy that he has not got the time. He is the owner of the business i.e. he was the Captain. I was to meet him at 10.30am at the unit on the following Wednesday with my camper.

I left bright and early, I had about a 2 hour drive. On nearing the trading estate I was unable to find their unit so I rang them. Mario answered, I said "Good morning I am near your unit but I cannot find it." He said "Well I am off to get some parts." I then said "I have an appointment with you at 10.30." There was a silence "Oh yes", it was quite obvious that he had forgotten. "Well I am not far away, I will be with you in a few minutes." "I said I am parked at the mobile café." "Ha I know where you are, just hang on there." Well I was not planning on driving off, as he had promised he soon found me and directed me to follow him. We arrived at their unit and I stepped out and shook hands with him. Mario aka Maz is a man of small stature with large oily boots and a woollen hat.

Firstly he dived under the back end of my camper immediately jumping back out at the same time informing me that it was fine, they could fit a TDI.

As we walked into the unit I was quite surprised at the amount of campers all at different stages of body repairs or replacement engines. Also the amount of parts strewn everywhere. I was introduced to Daz who was a tall chap with oily boots and a wool hat. He was the hands on man and did a great deal of the work on conversions himself. I certainly found them all very welcoming and comfortable to be with.

With a cup of tea thrust into my hand Mario then described the procedure when doing the conversion. We remove both engine and gear box and then we acquire a 1900 VW TDI engine. We then strip that engine and rebuilt it, he gave me a list of parts that automatically get changed plus anything that they may have doubts about. He then showed me a rebuilt engine and gear box, I was most impressed.

The gear box goes to Aidan Talbot in Wales. There the box is stripped and rebuilt with the necessary parts that need to be replaced, and the gear box bill comes directly from Aidan.

I asked "What happens to my old engine?" Mario replied with a smile "You can sell it, we do not want it." Who would? DAZ with his dry sense of humour then piped up and said "They were the next thing to steam." "Will it use any oil as I carry 2 gallons on a trip and use it?" "It may use a little until it all beds in then it will be fine, just carry a pint most lightly you will not need it."

It was some time after I had the new engine fitted that I finally believed him.

My next question was "When can you do it?" "Well it is going to be after Christmas", we were now in late October. "How long will you have it for?" "Usually about a month." I paid the deposit and was on my way.

A NEW INTERIOR CONVERSION

My next stop was a small camper conversion shop just outside Birmingham, this was to see Mark at Starlight Campers. My thoughts were that if I was going to have a new engine and gear box why not have a professional job done on the inside. After talking to Mark I decided to go ahead. He quoted me £2,000.00 and said that he wanted the van completely stripped out, plus I had to reline the floor. He said if I could get it back to him within a week I could have it back just before Christmas. I paid the deposit and was on my way.

ALL THE INTERIOR GONE ONCE AGAIN A VAN

The next couple of days my friend Maurice and I stripped her out. Maurice fitted a new floor, then because I had built a small fold away extension on the back of the camper we were given the extra space to build in more storage and also a space for a toilet. I will call the new toilet hedge as I have watered the best hedges all over the world. No more of that I will have a T25 with a toilet. How spoilt can one man be? I rewired the lights and sockets. Not much tea drinking went on, just banter as Maurice and I have a very similar sense of humour. I rang Mark and said it is ready. I arranged to deliver it the next day. I was able to arrange a lift home. My friend Adam had rang to say he could pick my bike up for a few repairs. Adams work shop was not far away from Starlight Campers so we arranged a time and he picked me up. When arriving home we loaded my bike and away he went, so that worked out very well.

O.k. it is all underway I can only hope it all works and fits in.

As promised I picked her up 3 days before Christmas and I was delighted with the result. It was finished so well and all lightweight materials were used. My biker friend Tabitha had taken me up to Birmingham so as we were quite early we took in the National Motorcycle Museum fitting in a little lunch at the same time.

MY TDI CONVERSION MARIO

Three weeks after Christmas, I delivered my camper to Mario. He said "It will be ready in about a month's time. I left them to it and did not ring him until the month was up. Mario answering the phone in his usual I do not want to talk to you but I will syndrome. "Ha glad you rang, we are waiting for the gear box and as soon as it is back we can start assembling. It did not sound like much progress had been made.

I did not question him as it was winter and I may not have been using her much. I then seemed to be getting some enthusiasm from Mario "While you are on the phone would you like the new type of injectors?" "I think they will give you a better performance." I readily agreed, so it was left like that.

Three weeks later I rang again. "Hello Mario how is my camper progressing?" "It is coming on very well, the engine and gear box are in we just have to link everything up." "It will be ready in two weeks time." A date was made to collect her and to say I was rather thrilled would be an understatement. The day arrived and as agreed we arrived at 10.30am. Well Mario saw me and he looked as if the world had just dropped away.

It turned out he had forgotten the date and also he had forgotten to finish the job. He proceeded to show me what had been done and also what had to be done. I was very disappointed but after a while I thought well it is nearly finished, so it will not be long now. On speaking to Daz he said "Did he say it would be ready today?" "Yes he did." Daz then explained that Mario was in shock, he had had a telephone call from the hospital 10 minutes before I arrived. His Wife had gone for a scan and she had just told him they were having twins.

TWINS AND A TDI CONVERSION

On leaving I congratulated him also saying "How you fitted that in I have no idea", a very weak smile came back. He followed me to my car. "Your camper will be ready soon, ring me in a weeks time." He wandered off with his tail between his legs. He is under a great deal of pressure but having got to know them all Mario is a very switched on chap, I did say to him on one of our meeting "You are pretty smart, his reply was "VW spent millions perfecting the TDI all I do is adapt it." For me I am not so sure I think he is very clever.

I had been hoping now to get away and find some sun. Jenny had been texting me with suggestions that we meet in Spain. I had replied saying that I was having problems with the van and was trying to get it fixed. I did not mention the new TDI Oooooh.

Just about a week later Mario rang me. We have had a few problems but it will be ready for you in two weeks' time. Oooh great but I readily agreed, what alternative did I have? A date was arranged and nearing that date I rang Mario and said "I can only get a lift to the Worcester Turning off the M5." It was agreed he would pick me up from there.

TODAY IS THE DAY, MAYBE NOT

The day finally came around. I arrived about 10.30am. Mario finally picked me up about 4pm, not in my camper as expected but in another van. He explained that they had a few problems and Daz was working on it at the moment. My view was that it just was not ready, but on arrival it all looked quite good, it was just missing its back wheels. I saw the tail end of Daz, his head well down and a few wires hanging here and there. On inquiring Daz said it was nearly there, so I wandered off to look at his own transporter that he was rebuilding in his spare time. What spare time, the poor lad seemed to be working all the time but having said that he had loads of new parts fitted, I would say why haven't I got one of those, I want one of these. I really loved the look of his engine.

Well with numerous cups of tea the evening wore on. I was having a long day and feeling very tired. I would have been quite happy to stay in a hotel near and come back in the morning, but now it looked like it would be completed.

WITH A SMILE SHE BURST INTO LIFE

Mario said "That's done." Daz replied "Yes" both with a smile, the engine turned over and burst into life. Ooh boy what a nice sound, it was music to my ears.

Mario was away off up the road and was back in ten minutes. He hopped out and conversed to Daz in some language I did not understand, it seemed adjustments were being made. Then a quick wipe over and down went the engine cover. "O.k. she is all yours." With many thanks and smiles I climbed in. I was away too tired to think of anything else but getting home. I really did not think of how it was performing, I just drove home, parked up and was soon settling down for a good night's sleep at last.

IN THE LIGHT OF DAY

The next morning I was keen to get out and have a daylight look at her. Immediately I noticed a trail of something on the road so it was engine cover up, the engine was running diesel from the fuel pump I tried all the screws but they were tight.

I then rang Mario explaining as best I could what I though was happening. His response was not what I expected. "O.k. I will be with you about lunch time." He was, with a few spare seals and rubber type rings. It was soon fixed. We took a late lunch, I found it very interesting as to how he started his business and what he was looking to do in the future also fitting in having babies. "Well enjoy your camper, you will have a smile from ear to ear." He was on his way.

I gave her a good spring clean. There were some oily marks on my new flooring but I persevered and soon she was gleaming.

OK NOW DRIVE
FAT ASS IS NOT IN MY VOCABULARY

The start-up was um a nice sound, then slipping into gear, this nice smooth gear box, then away 1-2-3-4-5 pulling like a train, realizing that once into top gear you have no reason to change down. The engine has so much torque, it was like driving a new van. I slipped onto the motorway running down the slip road accelerating with no effort, no peddling and no leaning forward to help it along. There was no swearing at her to get her fat ass into gear and go, just sit back and let it happen. Some months later I received a speeding ticket, I had flashed past a camera. It was the best sort of ticket one could receive, I did it in a 1988 VW T25, and you usual get pulled up for going too slow and being a hazard to other road users. Even worse was that cyclist passing me going uphill. Can you believe that? but not anymore. After a few days of running about I started to get lights coming up on the dash, first the oil then the water. Checking the levels I found them to be fine, so I made a phone call once again to Mario. The phone was answered in the usual way, I don't want to, but I will. I explained, he went quiet, he was thinking. "Um can you come up?" "I think I need to have a look, I'm not quite sure why that would happen." The next day I was away and arrived early. They were very busy but a cup of tea was thrust into my hand and I waited. Finally Mario got to it just after lunch, spending ten minutes on it then was called away to something else that was going on. On about the third or fourth go he announced that he had found the problem, lifting the unit that holds the clocks and switches, the fine printed circuit connections were very tarnished and had very obviously been cleaned up before this and this had made them wafer thin. The work shop turned into action everyone hunting for a set of clocks but the one we needed did not appear. It was agreed that I would try and find a set on the internet. I was dispatched with "They are very hard to find, good luck."

The drive from Telford is very nice so I slipped her into top and just enjoyed the drive. Ooh apart from the light popping on every now and then everything was fine, I will be happier when this is sorted out.

On arriving home I went to my computer and sat and searched but found nothing, so each day I sat and looked. After one week I went on again and low and behold two popped up. Oooh great, the first one was for a petrol model and the second one was a diesel. I clicked purchase. In three days it arrived.

MARIO

I was then off back to Telford and the boys. Mario went straight to it, unpicking the printed circuit. On removing the old one, he then gently proceeded to attach the new one. Within half an hour it was all back in place and running with no lights flickering on. I think he was as delighted as I was. Before leaving I arranged to have a cruise control fitted, "I will ring you when the parts arrive."

Some years later the call still has not come. Who wants a cruise control anyway? I left feeling very pleased with both their efforts and mine. With a wave from both of them I glided out of the trading estate and onto the open road. I slipped her into fifth gear and sat there enjoying my drive home.

JENNY

I had been receiving a few text messages from Jenny, she was back in the U.K. but gave no indication of wanting to meet up at any time. It was quite obvious to me that I had not been forgiven for the morning she had wasted hanging around for me while my camper was repaired.

Over the next few weeks I did a few excursions. One of my favourites was the West coast of Wales also Porlock was a great walking area. My camper was living up to all Mario had said.

PEMBROKESHIRE

My next trip was near Pembroke, a very nice beach and rocky coast line, great for walking and a swim if the water was warm enough. I had sent a text to Jenny who was responding in a very enthusiastic way. Um. I passed a few very posh and expensive campers on route, I just glided by them as they phoned there local dealer saying I have just paid £60,000.00 for a camper from you and an old VW has just passed me as though I was stood still. Oh what joy? There was no more slip streaming lorries for hundreds of miles to get a tow. Just pure power.

I settled into a little campsite that I had visited for many years. On the morning after a good breakfast I donned my walking boots and with my small pack consisting of water and a sandwich made from what was left over from breakfast, I set off. After walking for half an hour I came across a group who I think were planning to jump off the rocks into the sea. They were all quite young with no fear what so ever. They did ask if I would like to join them but after one second consideration I declined much to their disappointment. The three senior leaders smiled and said "Good decision." Then one of the leaders explained that they leap into the sea Oooh and it's a long way down. Then they picked up their canoes and paddled around the bay to where a vehicle could pick up the canoes, also bringing them lunch. It sounded great fun but I will give it a miss today but I was thinking about how nice it was to be asked anyway.

As the last one jumped, I watched as they gathered together and swam to the canoes. Soon they were all ready and off they went, I thought that if I walked back the way I come maybe I would see them again. First I ate my sandwich then headed off. I saw no sign of them, maybe they were in one bay while I was in another. I kept a look out until I had to take to the foot path leading back to the campsite rounding the gate at the campsite.

JENNY HAS FLOWN IN

I stopped, parked next to me was a very bright green camper with flowers. Well I'll go to sea it's got to be Jenny. Well it was, as I walked in between the campers she shot out and grabbed me, smothering me with quite a few kisses. Looks like a change of heart. Next a cup of tea was thrust into my hand, saying "We have so much to talk about." She was right I think we did.

Firstly "Your camper is a different green." "Yes I had a body job done on her after you told me it was looking shabby." "Did I say that?" "Yes you did" but having said that "How are your wheels doing?" "They are great thanks to you" she said. Looks like I did something right.

I then took my time relaying the saga of my engines, all three of them. She had difficulty getting her head around the Councillor who was such an ass until I revealed to him that I knew he was a Conservative Councillor.

We talked until both of us were running out of steam, so off to bed. The campers were parked so close I could shout "Good night" from my bed. I could hear the reply followed by a quite loud fart. Maybe the next thing to purchase were some ear plugs. "Good night."

The next morning I awoke to rain, so I made a cup of tea and settled down with my book. About eleven it was easing up and finally the sun started to warm my camper. I had no reason to dress and struggle across the field to the toilet now I have my own loo. It made my camper complete a 1900 VW TDI WITH A TOILET, what more could a man ask for? How posh is that?

About mid-day I heard some movement from next door and as the sun was now shining it was time to get up. On opening my side door to my surprise there was a table set for late breakfast or lunch. With a six foot leggy blond handing me my tea. Well this is nice. We chatted over breakfast and decided to go for a walk trying to keep to the shore. Looking at the map maybe we could do it, so with two bottles of water we were away. Do you know I think she may have left her broom at home. I was not allowed to do the washing up or was it that I was not allowed in the camper. I was not quite sure. I had shown her the new inside conversion on my camper, I think secretly she was a little envious.

WE STARTED WALKING

After a while we took to the shore path. It was very steep and I was thinking if you go down then you have to come back up. After walking for some time on the beach we came to the rocks. I though Jenny was more athletic than she seemed to be but without comment we worked our way over the rocks, finding little sandy bays, more rocks, more beaches until it became too hot so we sat for a while. Jenny seemed to be taking in the area around us, and to my surprise said "How about a swim." To me, yes it had turned into a lovely afternoon but it still looked a bit cold. "Well you wimp?" (There was no call for that) "I am going to swim" I said "Did you bring your swimmers?" She looked at me with that look. "If you are not coming then I am going behind that rock, so don't look." "Look at what", then came a scowl. I could see where this was leading because she had been checking out if we could be seen from the cliff tops. The shout went up "Look the other way" so briefly I did but as she ran to the water I though good lord she is a bit pale. That needs sorting out, maybe the south of France.

She struck out towards some rocks, so in seconds I was de robed and racing into the sea, Ooh when I hit the water Ooh boy it was cold, I just swam around. It was when she reached the rocks she turned around and with arms raised screamed and was on her way back, so I struck out for the shore. The next thing was a hand gripped my leg so I came to an abrupt halt. She admired my tan asking if it was all over. I said "You need to check it out." She slapped me and roared with laughter. We swam back to the shore just keeping our modesty below the water. She said "You get out first." "I am not getting out first, you get out first." Finally it was decided that with us both holding hands we would get out together and walk to our clothes. What this was intended to achieve I have no idea, we stood up together hand in hand looking straight ahead we walked to our clothes. Well she was looking straight ahead, I was not. There was a scrabble for our clothes and things went back to normal, if you could call it normal. She seemed to be a very modest lady. She was fine on our walk back, but the beach was not mentioned again that day but what was mentioned was that maybe she would move on this evening. Now I found that a bit over the top, it was all just because I had seen her white bum running down the beach. Instantly I said "Don't you think that is a bit silly, we are adults, we went for a swim that is all we did."

SHE RAN AGAIN

She started sobbing "I do not know what I want." "O.k. well let's have tomorrow together then go on our way." She happily agreed to that so while she was showering I walked to the local fish and chip shop for our dinner.

We sat and chatted enjoying the meal, both of us turned in quite early. She did shout "Good night", that was a bonus.

ON THE ROAD AGAIN

On awakening that morning I looked out and her camper had gone. No surprise there. Well that decision made I went about my morning, breakfast and a nice shower. I packed my lady and once again was away, smiling when I changed into fifth gear. What fun you are to drive.

SPITFIRE

I stopped off at an airdrome near Haverfordwest. There was a small Museum there with a WW2 spitfire in pieces, the intention was at some time to rebuild it and hopefully it would fly again. They are always looking for donations or you could take bits and pieces that they can sell. This spitfire was found in Australia and shipped back. In the last few years it had changed owners quite a few times. This visit I took a few books and some small aircraft parts I had collected over the years. This all goes one day I hope, to rebuilding this wonderful aircraft.

To complete my visit I wandered over to the café and devoured a sausage, bacon and egg sandwich. I am sure that's very good for you, well the tea was nice. It was then back to my power house, the smile returning as the big motor turned over and burst into life. I pointed her towards the M4 and sat in my wonderful fifth gear and let her take me home. Out of Haverfordwest, again a long steady climb towards St Clears. Ooh look some real posh campers ahead, thinking through my smile, I muttered "They are mine." Blue and I just sat there on the speed limit, gaining ground on them like a greyhound. Oh they have spotted me, one pulls out then another. These boys are going for it but with their heavy loads, some changing gear was done and having to move over for faster car traffic but before they could move out to block my way I purred past them accelerating and leaving them just a spot in my mirror, plus I have a toilet. Well they will have something to chat about this evening.

Onto the M4 around Port Talbot and onto the next services. I fuelled up then parked up and wandered over to the service area to use the facilities, saves me cleaning my loo. I wandered around the shops and bought a folding chair as mine has a tear in it. Then I walked in the direction of my camper. Oh stop, wait hang on, don't move, there were two very large campers parked across from old Blue, but the two male occupants were not by their campers one of them was on his back under the rear end of Blue. I concealed myself as best I could trying to catch what they were saying but I was just too far away. Their hand gestures were giving me enough information. After a good grovel around the car park they seemed none the wiser. Their hand gestures took over and well there they were, whoosh an arm went shooting forward, hand to his head looking into the distance. From what I could make out I think they wanted to ask me how come they may be paid £60 - £70 thousand pounds and my £2,000.00 worth just ate them up. I stayed hidden in the shrubbery until they decided to pop over to the toilets. As soon as they were out of sight I ran over, jumped in and was away just catching a Wife in my rear view mirror running after me. Being the gentleman I am I purred away onto the M4. The smile returned as I slipped her into fifth gear. O.K. let's go home.

HOME WITH MY SON AND MY FRIENDS

Life went back to normal, a little writing a little resting, a few more jobs around the house, plus a little bike riding mainly alone but occasionally with my friend Tabitha with her Honda firestorm, quite some bike. Tabitha is quite a rider and a pleasure to ride with. Our favourite trip was different routes to end up at Abergavenny, usually to chat with other bikers and sometimes a bacon butty and a cup of tea. Occasionally I sell a book or two.

MAKE HER AS SAFE AS POSSIBLE

My thoughts turned towards planning my next trip having promised my friends Toni and Sara that I would visit them in Spain. Also I was planning to meet up with Jenny. My first thoughts were about how easily they had broken into my camper, so I consulted a friend of mine who specialized in alarm systems. I really wanted something very loud so it was decided that we could fit two sirens one inside my camper and one underneath which also covered all doors and the extension part on the back of the camper. I was given the job of running in the cables. This was not easy as being 6ft and of average build getting my upper torso into the cupboards was not easy but with a lot of grunting and groaning I was ready for Nick to do the final connections. On testing it, it worked very well. We were both very pleased with our efforts. My next job was to make a safe for my computer. I needed to make it hard for someone to find it, so after working out a good place, I set to work with aluminium plate and twin locks. After the work was completed it took me five minutes to open the safe, this was by moving a few things and undoing the locks. Feeling happy with my camper I was ready to head to warmer climates.

FLYING TOWARDS SPAIN

Dover was my destination the first day, I like this crossing as it's just over an hour and you are away. If I can catch an early Ferry then I can usually motor on getting well under Paris and away south. My route when moving South is Calais - Rouen - Evreux - Chartres and Orleans, taking to the auto route that I now find is so easy to drive. I just cruise in my fifth gear, one of five Oooh. Towards evening I was in the area of Drew – Chartres. I believed I had at some time camped at Chartres and in no time I was seeing signs for the camping Municipal. The river Eure passes through Chartres and the signs were taking me in that direction. At Reception I was told to park anywhere. I paid the camp site fee, I find this a better move as at some sites if you pay when you leave they hold your passport. I am paranoid about my passport and like to keep it with me.

I parked up, quite close to me was another camper with English plates. After putting the kettle on I put my chair out to take in the last of the evening sun and was soon into a conversation with my neighbours. They were travelling north after their first adventure with their camper and going as far as Southern Spain. They were so full of the trip, but they had had a very bad experience, their camper was broken into but fortunately they had an alarm of sorts. It seemed just a few things were grabbed and they made a run for it. Their computer was fine, it was in their little safe, so they were not too upset about it but they had become more cautious as to where they parked and how they left the van. What seems to have happened is they stopped at a super market and both went in. They had noticed a few undesirables hanging around but that seemed normal these days, but they did not think anything of it. In fact they did not hear the alarm when they were in the super market. They came out and yes the half-light was broken. A few things were gone, the satnav, one phone, one iPad that had been left lying around (in case they were broken into) as it had not worked for ages, their towels that were drying across the dash board and a few cloths.

As I had they went to the police station. They spent 3 hours there filling in forms and doing whatever. Nothing was ever recovered, also their Insurance Company fought them tooth and nail. Why do we have to pay insurance?

It had been great chatting to them but now it was time for bed, wishing them good travels I settled down for the night.

WARM

The morning was bright and the warmth was radiating through my little camper. After a cuppa I set off south, hold up there was a note under my wiper. Having retrieved it I discovered it was their address and email. How nice was that?

I had decided to have a slow day not moving far but the road conditions were good so I just enjoyed the DRIVING, TDI. I arrived North of Perpignan in the late evening just in time to catch the pizza shop. I had visited this site in the past so I was happy to settle for a week as the weather was glorious. I was allocated a nice corner pitch, and soon settled in, having devoured the pizza on my way to find the pitch. (Bit peckish I think). I set up my little camper and off to bed.

SUN SEA AND SAND

Plus it's warm.

Wow, was it warm when I crawled out in the morning. I first put my mosquito nets to the two side windows, then put up my net that completely covered my bed. A cup of tea, an egg sandwich and I was ready to face the day. I texted Jenny just in case she was around as I had heard nothing since our meeting in Wales.

My plan today was to start walking the coast line. I set off with my map, water bottle and sun hat. My plan was to walk on the water's edge, not always easy but I will give it a go. I walked for about 2 miles of beach then the rocks loomed up ahead so very slowly I started around the rocks quite often taking to the sea. I ended up swimming so my nice map got quite wet as did my vintage shorts and tea shirt. Tomorrow I will bring a plastic bag to put my clothes in, then after swimming I can put my clothes back on. It was so warm today that walking in wet gear was quite a pleasure. I also found about 6 pieces of sea glass. I have been collecting it for years, some coastal areas are better that others. Near fisherman's huts seem to be great places. I think for years they threw their wine bottles into the sea. Every piece I have found has been rolling around in the sea for years, there are also many colours.

Mid-afternoon and I had covered very little ground as the sea was so inviting that I swam and sunned myself. I think it was about time to find a cliff path. I had seen one a little ways back so I headed for that one. Well it may have been a cliff path but it was steep. When I finally made it I sat resting before moving on.

Well the walk back to the camp site was easy finding a good path across the cliff top.

I picked up some eggs and bread at the shop on the camp site, making my way back to my camper. The site seemed pleasantly quiet. I was looking forward to the showers as they have always been great i.e.

hot. Even with the weather being so warm I love to soak under a warm shower. My towel that I had draped over the bonnet was good, dry and very warm so I wandered to the showers and had a very nice relaxing shower. I should have a shave but not today.

JENNY

Walking back to Blue I noticed some movement, in fact a chair was sitting next to my door. As I approached it, someone stepped out. It was Jenny, she threw her arms around me in a wonderful embrace.

"Hey how did you know I would be here?" "Because you told me you always head for this site." Well I cannot remember telling her that. "I only texted you this morning." "I know I must have been following your route through France." She said "Well it is wonderful to be here and the weather is so good." That was rather a nice response from Jenny, she can be very nice but at times very feisty. Well just enjoy it, maybe she left her broom at home this time. I said "I have eggs and bread would you like to help me eat it?" "NO you are coming to me for dinner this evening." "Well no, that is not all together right, I am bringing my camper to you and parking there", pointing to the area next to Blue. "O.K. fine by me." She arrived in no time, parked up and set to with the cooking. She seemed to know a lot about me because I kept thinking, did I tell her that. This evening she cooked my favourite, fish (well conger eel). She had taken the meat off of it after cooking and made a sauce that looked wonderful.

I had no wine, but a bottle of my favourite came onto the table. Two glasses loosens the tongues and we chatted away. I told her how pleased I was with my new engine rebuild and what fun I have driving her. She in turn had returned home (to date she had not revealed where home was) but come to think about it neither had I. (what a nice odd friendship).

She was very impressed with my mosquito net over my bed, so was I as I dislike the little tykes with a vengeance.

I told her that I was walking the coast and had started today, well hopefully I was. I told her about my jaunt today so I will be wandering for a few days. She said "Not on your own, I am coming with you." Well this was a shock to me. I did not mention the plastic bag thing I just said I had to swim a bit. She then said "Could we start again in the morning?" "What do you mean?" "Well start off where you started today." "Well o.k. that's a great idea", at least I would know where I was going.

At that I walked her back to her camper 3 metres away. "O.k. sleep tight." At that point she came forward saying with tears streaming down her face "I am so sorry how I behaved to you in Wales but I am so mixed up." She unloaded the lot on me. Men had been a big problem. This came about after she finally left her husband. He had lost his possessions and had not given up treating her badly, interfering with her life for many years. Fortunately her two children who were in their late teens had stayed with her until departing for University. Then with selling her house and getting a smaller home she was able to start fulfilling her dreams and travel with her T25. I think the camper is also to put space between her and her ex-husband. She is still quite screwed up.

Well time for bed. A passing "Good night" was proceeded by "I am a total mess and my ex-husband is a total ass hole." Well that seems about right.

SUN SHINE

Morning arrived with lovely sunshine and warmth. After my morning cuppa I legged it to the small market and bought a small cooked ham (well I think that was what it was) plus half a Melon. Back to the campsite, and there was no sign of movement from next door. I sat and devoured the melon and made the sandwiches. Then after some concentrated banging about, opening and closing doors I decided to make a start, water, plastic bag by 2. I left a note under her wiper. It read I have gone to the beach, I will wait for an hour then I am off on my walk. All locked up, I was away. Having reached the beach it was wonderful that no one was about. I could not resist it and went straight into the sea after laying out my plastic bag. Ooh was that nice or what?

I ran out dropping down on the sand to sun myself and dry off. By this time Jenny was the last thing I was thinking about. Having just put my shorts and tee shirt on I heard a shout and there she was steaming across the sand. She reached me in a bath of sweat and dropped onto the sand. After about five minutes she began to recover and launched into me telling me how mean I was for going off without her. She said "I heard you banging the doors." "O.K. then why did you not get up?" "Because I was comfortable." There was no answer to that.

"O.k. look you are here so how about we have a nice day." Having calmed her down she gave me a nice smile and said "Sorry." By this time it was very hot so walking was slow but the scenery was taking over the little bays that I had experienced yesterday. Then we came around the head land. "It is time for a swim." She stopped abruptly and said "What, we do, now? I reached into my bag and pulled out a plastic bag "Put your clothes in that and swim to that point about 50 metres away."

Her mouth opened with a barrage of protests. Instantly I said with venom "Shut up." I walked behind a rock and put my shorts and tee shirt in the plastic bag. I walked into the sea and started swimming to the next bay. During all this I had not looked at her once.

I reached the rock and climbed onto the beach. I put my DRY clothes on and waited. She appeared dragging her plastic bag behind her. She came out of the water with a big grin on her face. "Sorry I am a mess." "Please do not keep saying sorry to me, just enjoy your day." "Tell me did you ever do this, i.e. walking the coast." "NO." "O.K. well enjoy it." She put her shorts on, that was it, (I was not unhappy about that) we walked on. It was nearing time to eat so after about half an hour we came to the beach I had loved yesterday, finding a nice rock to sit by. I produced my plastic bag and went into the sea. As I hit the water I was passed by Jenny screaming at the top of her voice. "This is wonderful." Well I had told her that.

After cooling down a bit we sat, eating my sandwiches with Jenny going into raptures of how wonderful this was, I hope it goes on forever. I was wondering had she realized that her clothes were still sunning themselves where she had dropped them. But a few minutes later she said "I have never done this before." "Done what before?" "Been swimming with no clothes on." "O.K. are you enjoying it?" At that she rolled over and kissed me. Oooh that's nice, just as I was thinking how relaxed she was, she jumped up and raced into the sea with me hot in pursuit.

Our day continued, it was so nice to see her so relaxed and me for once having a pal. That afternoon I think we swam, walked, searched for glass, it seemed to me we both so much enjoyed being together. Maybe she will not run off this time.

We then found the cliff path and both of us struggled to reach the top. We both collapsed in a heap when we finally arrived at the top.

This is when we first saw people so the shorts and tee shirt were in place. I think she was enjoying her dream. It is France so why not?

We stopped off at the shop for bread and a bottle of wine. It was my turn to cook so it was the cold wonderful cooked ham, bread and butter. The wine was in my little fridge so really all was ready. While this was going on Jenny was taking her time having a shower, what do women do in bathrooms? I legged it to the shower, in, out all done and back at the camper. Still there was no sign of my beach combing friend. I opened the bottle of wine and sat quietly taking in the day and what a wonderful day we were having. I was brought from my dreams by a tall leggy blond dressed in a towel with her hair draped over her shoulders. Well she had been so long in the shower but what had returned was a very nice blond dressed in only a towel. We sat in the cool of the evening, there was not much to say as we had chattered all day. We ate quietly, it seemed we were both dreaming. Jenny poured the last of the wine, as she handed me my glass she held on to me and with a gentle smile she whispered "Shall we go to bed? I simply said "Yes." Two campers, only one that evening with a light on, we cuddled up under my mosquito net and the light went out.

BLISS

For the next few weeks we walked the coast, searched for glass, lay in the sun, we swam and made love on every part of the coast. We both loved sea food, we had found some Oyster shacks and made regular visit. Always swimming in the sea on our way back, rolling in the surf, just enjoying being together.

I had talked a little about my friends in Spain. I had an open invitation to visit them at any time. I had stayed many times, Sara's husband Tony was one of the nicest men I have ever met, he was softly spoken and a very sincere man, I got on with him so well. How could you not like them? They were great together and so in love. Sara I had met a few years earlier on a plane flying back to the U.K. I had been relaying stories of the boy's bike trip that we try and do every year. She let it slip that they have a Honda Africa twin, instantly I said "So have I." She said "My Son is very much into off roading and he would love to join you." I did manage to sell her a book at the same time. Well her Son did come with us. It was great having him, we had so much fun, plus as we were in Spain his Spanish was excellent. (Helpful I would say). He only told us later on that he had not got a driver's license.

MOVING SOUTH AGAIN

It was decided that we would leave Jenny's camper on the site and make for the Costa Brava for a few days. Oooh this rocket ship I now drive will certainly impress her (no it didn't) must be a female thing, she probably got bored of my commentary on the virtues of a Mario conversion but when I am impressed then there is no stopping me.

I ran through the facts of her performance as we galloped uphill passing everything imaginable and smiling at the same time, flying over the Spanish boarder. What a dream, a fast VW T25 with a toilet and a 6ft leggy blond. Some boys are just spoilt.

SARA TONY

We arrived and were greeted as if I had only just seen them yesterday. I introduced Jenny and immediately we all got on so well. How could we not? Jenny was a little taken aback because Tony was preoccupied with de fleeing their little dog. It seemed to be working, they were jumping everywhere. I did pop into the camper and gave myself a good spray of the mosquito stuff. I was closely followed by Jenny who said "You can see them jumping." They did not jump for long. I think Tony got the upper hand of them. I think he may have drowned them with some sort of oil, could have been Castrol, but I think not.

As soon as we arrived Sara had said "You are not sleeping in the camper I have prepared the tree house." Well I knew this well as I had stayed there before. She lead us across the bridge, Ooh she had made a great deal of effort it looked wonderful. Sara said "See you at eight for dinner" and disappeared. Jenny walked around, then stood looking at the sea in the distance, she was sobbing quietly. She said "Why didn't you tell me about this?" "They are wonderful, this is wonderful." I passed her the glass of wine that Sara had left for us. She did give me one of those looks (I am going). This was the first one in over six weeks but this time she could not go as her camper was in France. We went in and led on the bed both falling asleep. It seemed in no time there was a shout "Dinner." Quickly gathering ourselves off we went, Tony is a great cook and we had a wonderful evening. At the same time plans were made to ride out and do some of the roads where they met ten years ago for the second time.

Sara had been on holiday with her parents from a young age. This was when she first met Tony but as always in life, holidays stopped, work took over and family. Both Sara and Tony had married and had children but again as sometimes in life, things do not always go well. After her divorce Sara decided to visit Spain and look for Tony. One morning Sara was walking down a familiar street they both had memories of and Tony drove by in his pickup. Well he did not drive by he stopped. He was divorced and they had ten wonderful years together.

After a wonderful night Sara delivered us our breakfast onto our balcony and tapped the door as she left. Again we sat outside it was warm, it was nice. Sometimes dreams do come true.

Mid-morning we were ready for the off, we had the Africa twin and Tony and Sara were on a big V twin, I think it is a Kawasaki Drifter Indian Replica. I have no idea where they took us but the coast road was a biker's road very twisty and very much fun. Looking at my map it was the road to Sant Feliu. If I had time to look it was very scenic. We stopped for lunch in the small town of Tossa de Mar enthusing on our ride, the roads and the pleasure.

We then headed for home passing some crazy donkey in a field who when he heard a motor bike made a mad dash to the bottom of his field making a great deal of noise at the same time. We arrived early evening, tired but happy.

After a wonderful four days we said our goodbyes and once again we were on our way. We had decided to look at the coastal area and stay a couple of nights before returning to Jenny's camper. After driving the coast for a few miles we found a few small roads hoping they led to the beaches. We found one. I think you are allowed to stay wild camping for just 2 days. Again this was wonderful in the mornings, we crawled out and stepped into the sea. This was all we did for two days, just slept, ate and swam. Also it seemed a great area for sea glass so I managed to fit that in.

Jenny seemed to be getting edgy, she had been getting quite a few text messages but had said nothing to me. I believe it was pressure from her family but I was not really sure. Leaving this wonderful weather and our wonderful wild camp we moved north. We were now into October but still the weather was great. My thoughts were to stay while the weather held. We dropped into our oyster shacks to have six oysters and a glass of wine but the conversation seemed to lose its momentum. There was something going on that I did not know about. It seemed to me she was carrying some sort of guilt.

After settling on our camp site Jenny said "Can we walk the first part of our special walk tomorrow?" "Yes, great why not?" "I will pop to the market and get something for our lunch also we will need water." "O.K." I set off. Jenny wandered off to the shower while I went to the shop for pizza. When I got back she was not back so I went for a shower and back to the campers. Still no sign of her so I decided enough was enough so I opened the wine. Just as the cork came out she appeared looking nice and just wearing a towel.

So we sat and talked about all the things we had been doing. We drank the bottle and there was little left of the pizza. Sorry this wonderful day was coming to a close we snuggled under my mosquito net.

SORRY SEEMS SO EASY

As planned I was off to the market in the morning. I was gone about an hour, I wandered on to the campsite, I stopped Jenny's camper had gone. I somehow knew this would happen. There was a note on my camper it read "I am so sorry." Again, sorry seems so easy. She was gone.

We will meet again. With this in mind I stayed until the weather changed and then happily moved North with a smile on my face as I dallied in my VW TDI and home.

Mark Cheney.

EPILOGUE

Shortly after completing this third instalment of the "Horizon" series, Mr. Cheney began feeling short of breath, and not quite as fit as usual. After undergoing a series of tests, he received the devastating diagnosis: mesothelioma, the most lethal form of lung cancer, caused by exposure to asbestos in his early days as an electrician.

Knowing his time was short, he and his family sprang into action to ensure his remaining time on earth would be counted amongst his greatest adventures. He took a week-long holiday. His eldest son and his wife came over from America. He married his beloved girlfriend of over 20 years. Together with his younger son, daughter-in-law and a few close friends, he organised a party attended by over 100 of his closest family and friends from all over the world. There he expressed his gratitude for all their love and support over the years, and bade them farewell. He succumbed to his illness just 5 days later, less than 5 weeks after his diagnosis.

Mark has touched many lives over his 73 years, as a partner, father, father-in-law and grandfather, as a son and a brother, as a friend and a confidante. He was a big personality, with a warm heart and a generous soul. He has delighted many with his companionship, his stories and his love. His funeral was attended by nearly 300 of these grateful individuals whose lives he impacted.

So, this concludes Mark's adventures, as he has indeed finally found the horizon.

Ride in peace, Mark.

www.ingramcontent.com/pod-product-compliance
Lightning Source LLC
Chambersburg PA
CBHW060536100426
42743CB00009B/1545